RAILSCAPES

RAILSCAPES

A Northern Pacific Brasspounder's Album

Jim Fredrickson

WSU PRESS

Washington State University Press
Pullman, Washington

WASHINGTON STATE UNIVERSITY

Washington State University Press
PO Box 645910
Pullman, WA 99164-5910
Phone: 800-354-7360
Fax: 509-335-8568
E-mail: wsupress@wsu.edu
Web site: wsupress.wsu.edu

First printing 2003

Library of Congress Cataloging-in-Publication Data

Fredrickson, Jim.
Railscapes : a Northern Pacific brasspounder's album / Jim Fredrickson.
p. cm.
ISBN 0-87422-272-9 (hardbound : alk. paper)—ISBN 0-87422-271-0 (pbk. : alk. paper)
1. Railroads—United States—Pictorial works. 2. Railroads—United States—History.
3. Northern Pacific Railroad Company—History. I. Title.

TF23.F73 2003
385'.09795'022—dc21 2003013478

175 YEARS WSU PRESS
Fine Quality Books from the Pacific Northwest

Photo by Caryn Lawton

Shown here are a few volumes from "The Railroad Series" by Allen Chapman, held in a private collection by one of Jim's many friends, Ken Vogel of Pullman, Washington. Featuring a young man named Ralph Fairbanks, these books were popular with Jim and thousands of other youngsters in the decades prior to World War II. The first in the series, *Ralph of the Roundhouse* (subtitled *Bound to Become a Railroad Man*), was published in 1906, and the first few pages read like a near-parallel of Jim's early association with railroads:

> He appeared to know everybody, and to be a general favorite with every one, for the brakeman at the coach-end air brake gave him a cheery: "Hi, there, kid!" gaunt John Griscom, the engineer, flung him a grim but pleased nod of recognition, and the fireman, discovering him, yelled a shrill: "All aboard, now!"

Others in the ten-volume series bore such titles as *Ralph in the Switchtower*, *Ralph on the Engine*, *Ralph on the Overland Express*, *Ralph on the Midnight Flyer*, and *Ralph on the Mountain Division*. Obviously, Jim wasn't the only youngster enthralled by railroads, but over the decades he has been privileged to capture on film the mystique and potency of the magnificent puffing, pulling, and pushing world of trains.

—WSU Press

Table of Contents

Observation and Lounge Cars

In a Northern Pacific publicity photo from the late 1920s, a group of passengers pose on the open observation platform. This was a marvelous way to view the spectacular NP scenery, but there was a drawback: dust and cinders were kicked up when the train was moving at high speed. This could be called the "signature car" of the train—almost all observation cars sported an illuminated drumhead indicating the name of the train.

Photo from Steve Spalding collection.

A Luxurious Hotel on Wheels

"A Luxurious Hotel on Wheels" is how *Popular Science Monthly* magazine, in its July 1926 issue, described the ten observation lounge cars recently purchased by Northern Pacific for the *North Coast Limited.* The article featured several interior photos and a cut away diagram. It went on to say:

> This new type of railway car provides all the luxuries of the modern hotel for the traveler by rail. Within a total length of eighty-three feet, these remarkable cars provide lounge rooms, card rooms, shower baths for both men and women, a fully equipped soft drink parlor, a barber shop, valet service and observation platform.
>
> Startling innovations in railway car design were necessary to provide space for so many luxuries. Ordinary car doors and steps have been eliminated. The only entrance to the car is by way of the Pullman to which it is coupled. The space ordinarily used for vestibules is put to other service. The shower baths are supplied by an air pressure water system with tanks of 350 gallon capacity.
>
> Great pains have been taken to get rid of any similarity in appearance to ordinary chair cars. The seats in the lounge rooms and all of the decorations are individual in design. Each lounge contains a phonograph, library and other comforts.
>
> And for a final touch of luxury, a powerful electric searchlight has been fitted over the observation platform making sight seeing possible at night.

This luxury did not come without a price. The observation cars were strictly for the use of first-class passengers in the Pullman sleeping cars. A first-class ticket was considerably more pricey than the fare paid by those who rode in the day coaches. Generally, a "name" train was made up with a baggage car first behind the engine, then the day coaches and tourist sleeping cars, followed by the diner. Behind the diner were the Pullman sleeping cars, and at the rear was the observation car. My early trips on the *North Coast Limited* were during the Depression when we had barely enough money to buy a coach ticket. On occasion, I did try to sneak back to the observation car, but was politely turned back with the admonition, "Only first class Pullman passengers to the rear of the diner." It was very disappointing.

A Luxurious Hotel on Wheels

Barber Shops and Soda Fountains Are Provided in New Type of Railway Car

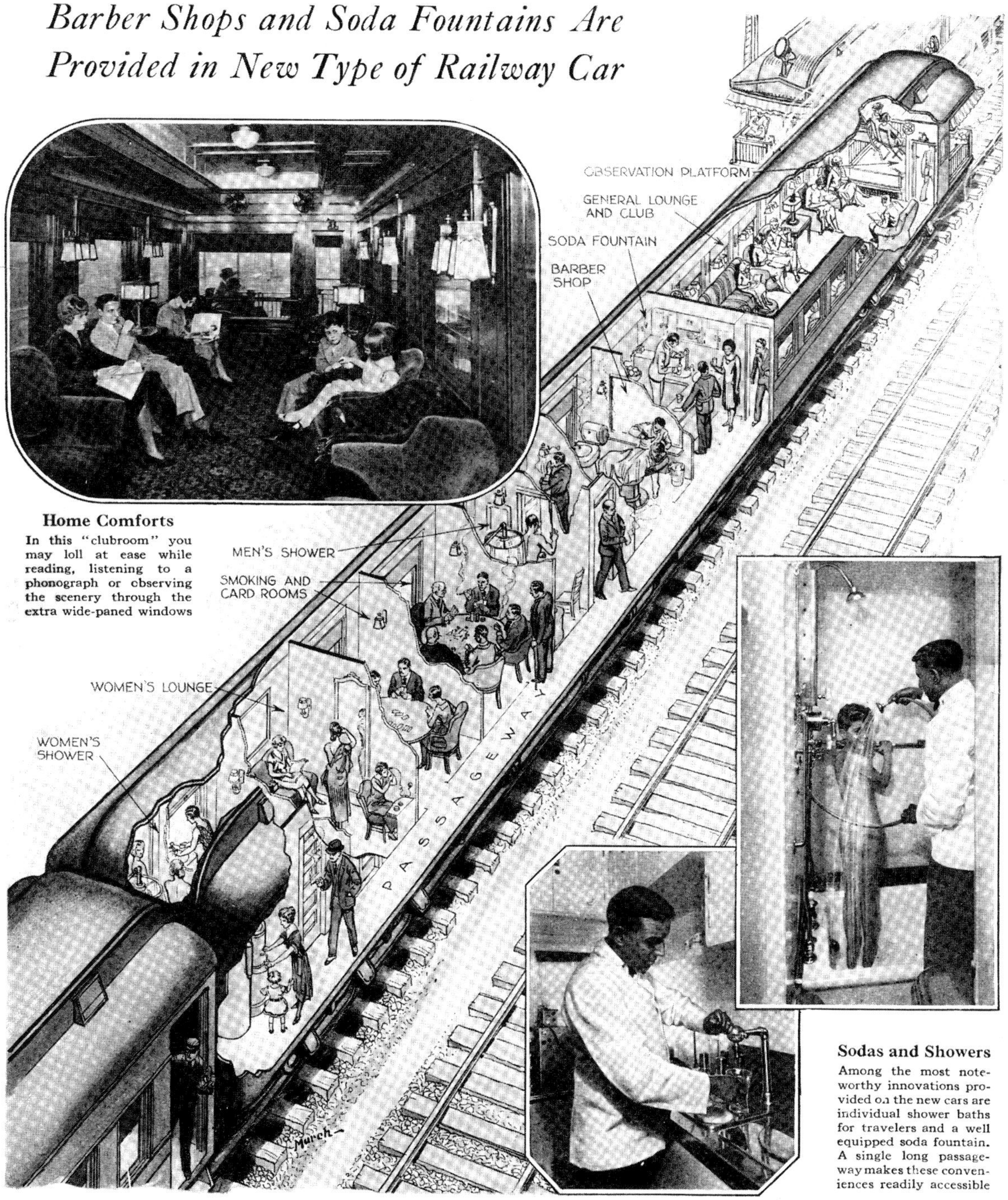

Home Comforts

In this "clubroom" you may loll at ease while reading, listening to a phonograph or observing the scenery through the extra wide-paned windows

Sodas and Showers

Among the most noteworthy innovations provided on the new cars are individual shower baths for travelers and a well equipped soda fountain. A single long passageway makes these conveniences readily accessible

All but one of the magnificent observation lounge cars were sold to the United States Army in 1943, just before I went to work for the Northern Pacific. They were rebuilt into hospital cars to transport wounded soldiers in World War II. The Northern Pacific replaced them with Pullman-owned Solarium cars, which had bedrooms and a lounge section at the rear, but no observation platform. The drumhead with the Monad trademark was replaced by a small metal *North Coast Limited* sign. One of these cars brings up the rear of the Pullman sleeper section of the *North Coast Limited,* passing by the section foreman's house at Martin, Washington, in 1944.

Rear of Solarium car *Grand Canyon* at King Street coach yard in Seattle, May 1945, showing its rather plain *North Coast Limited* sign. *Grand Canyon* contained three compartments, one drawing room, a buffet, and a 20-seat observation lounge.

Almost immediately after the war ended, NP joined most of the nation's railroads in the streamliner era, beginning construction on a new fleet of cars for the *North Coast Limited.* Six "round end" observation-lounge cars were included in the order. The old-style observation platform disappeared from virtually all railroads. The new cars were given names of prominent clubs along Northern Pacific routes—*Tacoma Club, Rainier Club, Arlington Club, Spokane Club, Montana Club,* and *Minneapolis Club*. This photo from May 28, 1952, shows *Minneapolis Club* on train Number 1, the westbound *North Coast Limited*, at Livingston, Montana, ready to begin the climb over Bozeman Pass and then the Continental Divide at Homestake Pass near Butte. Pullman passengers would be treated to spectacular scenery from comfortable lounge seats.

In November 1952, the Northern Pacific cut 12 hours from the running time of the *North Coast Limited* and commissioned famed designer Raymond Loewy to create a new look for NP's premier streamliner. Number 26, the eastbound *North Coast Limited*, with observation lounge 394, makes its important station stop for Yellowstone Park tourists at Livingston, Montana, on June 8, 1955. The original paint scheme has been replaced by what Northern Pacific aficionados dub "Loewy green": dark above the white stripe and light below. *North Coast Limited* lounge and sleeping cars originally had names; 394 formerly was *Montana Club.* Mr. Loewy apparently believed that numbers were more stylish than names.

As a lifelong resident of Tacoma, Washington, my favorite *North Coast Limited* car was 392—originally named *Tacoma Club*. It is seen here on the *North Coast Limited* at East Auburn early in 1953, sporting the new "Loewy green." After 19 years of service, the round-end observation cars fell victim to change. Northern Pacific replaced them with "Lounge in the Sky" buffet-sleepers: Vista Dome sleeping cars refurbished with tables in the domes for beverage service. The displaced rear cars were sold and, happily, *Tacoma Club*/392 began a new and prosperous life. It is now the observation lounge car on the *Sierra Madre Express*, running from Nogales on the Mexican border just south of Tucson, Arizona, to the wondrous Copper Canyon. I had the good fortune to be the escort for a Rail Travel Center tour group on this train and it was a real thrill to be aboard my favorite car again. It now carries the name *Arizona,* as shown in the photo taken at Posada, Chihuahua, Mexico, on January 1, 2000. I had photographed the interior of 392 at Seattle in 1955 and now had another chance near Benjamin Hill, Sonora, Mexico, on January 1, 2000. This time, with the advantage of using a tripod and self-timer, I included myself in the photo.

I always enjoyed riding in rear observation lounges or Vista Domes, and listening to people from the flatlands *ooohh* and *aaahh* about our marvelous Cascade scenery. These two views of Number 26, the eastbound *North Coast Limited,* were taken at Martin, Washington, just after the train emerged from the two-mile-long Stampede Pass Tunnel.

Below: On February 2, 1960, observation lounge 392, formerly *Tacoma Club*, is passing a rocky crag with a lonesome tree somehow growing from it. *Right:* On April 15, 1961, the Martin section foreman is giving Number 26 with the 390, originally *Rainier Club*, a roll-by inspection as it passes under the signal bridge.

The photos opposite and above illustrate a mysterious difference in the striping at the rear. 390 is the only observation lounge to have worn a broad stripe for most of its life on the Northern Pacific (another car had one for a short time). The reason for the different striping is unclear. Northern Pacific Historical Association member (and American Airlines pilot) Bill Kuebler addresses the subject exhaustively in his superb book, *The Vista Dome North Coast Limited.*

Over the PA system, stewardess nurses alerted passengers in lounge or dome cars to look to the rear for this striking view of the Stampede Tunnel snowshed at Martin and the waterfall behind it.

Dome Cars

By the 1940s, diesel-electric locomotives, particularly those built by the Electro-Motive Division of General Motors, were rapidly replacing steam engines on the nation's railroads. In 1944, EMD sent one of its executives, Cy Osborn, to report first-hand on the Denver and Rio Grande Western's freight movements through the Colorado Rockies. This assignment required him to ride in the cab of the diesel locomotive, allowing an unobstructed view of the stunning scenery. One day, while following the Colorado River through Glenwood Canyon, he began to think how wonderful it would be if travelers on passengers trains could have such a spectacular view of the scenery. On returning to GM's Electro-Motive headquarters in LaGrange, Illinois, he took his idea to the engineering department. As a result, the engineers built a model of a Domeliner passenger train. They showed it to various railroads, but wartime restrictions prevented any immediate construction of such cars. The Chicago, Burlington and Quincy, however, was quite taken with Mr. Osborn's vision and in 1945 rebuilt one of its streamlined coaches, the 4714, placing a glass-enclosed seating area above the roof line. Named *Silver Dome,* it was the first of the modern "Vista Dome" cars.

Mr. Osborn's idea turned into a smashing success. Over the next 13 years, 236 dome cars were built for more than 30 railroads in the United States and Canada. When Amtrak was created in 1971, it continued using them until changing over to Superliner-style cars.

Silver Dome was used primarily on CB&Q's *Twin Cities Zephyr,* but, when Amtrak shuffled the cars it inherited from the railroads, the *Silver Dome* found its way to Seattle where I photographed it in 1972. When it was retired by Amtrak in 1976, it was sold to the Mad River & NKP Museum in Bellevue, Ohio, where it remains as a tribute to a glorious era in railroad passenger service.

Among the noteworthy Vista Dome trains were the *California Zephyr* that ran from Chicago to Oakland over the Chicago, Burlington and Quincy, the Denver and Rio Grande Western, and the Western Pacific. The Rio Grande erected a monument to the dome car in Glenwood Canyon where the concept was born. This monument has since been moved to the Colorado Railroad Museum in Golden.

Train of Tomorrow

In 1945, after General Motors began conceptualizing glass-enclosed domes above the roof line of railroad passenger cars, a scale model was built and shown to more than 350 top railroad executives, who added ideas and suggestions. General Motors then ordered a four-car "Astra Dome"* train from Pullman Standard Car Manufacturing Company, to be powered by a 2,000 HP Electro-Motive diesel. Named *Train of Tomorrow,* it was delivered in May 1947 and sent on a 65,000-mile exhibition tour. (CB&Q had already built the first modern dome car—the *Silver Dome*—in 1945.) The *Train of Tomorrow* tour started in the Midwest on the Monon (Chicago, Indianapolis and Louisville) and reached the Pacific Northwest in December 1947. By this time it had been inspected by one million people in forty cities throughout the country. It arrived in Portland on the Southern Pacific and, after exhibition on December 4, 5, and 6, was handled by Northern Pacific crews to Tacoma and Seattle, with stops at Kelso, Centralia, and East Olympia to pick up press passengers. Gordy Stephens was the conductor, Charlie Everest the engineer, and Don Miller the fireman. One unique feature of its routing was movement via the American Lake Line (Fort Lewis) and South Tacoma so that the train would be facing in the desired direction when it backed into Tacoma Union Station.

When it was ready to leave Tacoma, I went down with my Graflex press-type camera in hand and boldly said to the attendant standing at the vestibule, "I'm with the Northern Pacific." He replied, without asking for credentials (which I didn't have), "The Press Office is in Bedroom D." Granted, I used a bit of subterfuge, but the ride was worth the risk.

Visitors were given a colorful brochure describing each car:

> STAR DUST
> This ultramodern chair car accommodates 72 persons in complete comfort. It is equipped with gloriously restful reclining seats. The 3 rooms under the Astra Dome are semi-private, ideal for family traveling. Spacious overhead luggage racks, rubber flooring under seats and heavily carpeted aisle complete the picture of travel luxury at moderate cost.
>
> SKY VIEW
> This car provides table seating for 18 passengers in the Astra Dome, 24 in the main dining room and 10 more in the private dining rooms on the lower deck. The Astra Dome offers all the advantages of roof garden dining—fine food, glamorous atmosphere, superb view.
>
> DREAM CLOUD
> The luxurious sleeping car, accommodating 20 passengers, includes 3 compartments under the Astra Dome, 2 drawing rooms at the forward end, and 8 duplex roomettes at the rear. They are furnished with such comforts of home as full-length wardrobes and mirrors. Matchless daytime comfort is provided by full-size lounges, restful chairs, and the space to enjoy them in privacy.
>
> MOON GLOW
> For friendly relaxation, there are 2 cocktail lounges furnished much like their counterparts in the smart supper clubs. There is a writing desk in a semi-private nook; telephone service is available to your home or business. The rear observation compartment affords a magnificent view of the swiftly changing landscape, through wide picture windows.

After the tour, the train was sold to the Union Pacific and in 1950 became part of the consists of its Portland to Seattle trains 457 and 458, until the early 1960s. *Moon Glow* was rescued from a scrapyard by the Golden Spike Railroad and Locomotive Society in Utah and is in storage, awaiting restoration. The remainder of the original Astra Dome cars were scrapped.

*Various railroads used different names for their dome cars. "Vista Dome" was the most common, but other names included: "Great Domes" on the Great Northern, "Pleasure Domes" on the Santa Fe, "Strata Domes" on the Baltimore and Ohio, and "Scenic Domes" on the Canadian Pacific.

GM's "Train of Tomorrow" on exhibition tour in Seattle, December 1947.

July 1954 was an exciting and joyful month for the Northern Pacific. The first of ten new Vista Dome coaches had been received from the Budd Company and soon would be in service on the *North Coast Limited*, giving the NP a major competitive advantage over its rivals, the Great Northern, Milwaukee Road, and Union Pacific.

To promote public awareness of this superb new service, two Vista Dome coaches, the 550 and 552, were sent to the Tacoma Division for exhibition at key cities. The first to arrive was the 550, which was displayed at Yakima on July 27 and 28. It then made its way to Ellensburg on train Number 5 for the public to inspect on the afternoon of the 28th and morning of the 29th. The Yakima-Cle Elum Local was instructed to be on hand to switch the car off and onto Number 5 on those two days. This provided a marvelous opportunity to photograph something very old and something very new together. (In another three years steam engines would vanish from regular use on the Northern Pacific.) From Ellensburg, 550 went on to Tacoma and then back to Seattle for public viewing before entering service on August 16.

An additional dome coach, 549, was purchased by the Northern Pacific in 1957. Of the original ten, two were owned by the Chicago, Burlington and Quincy and one by the Spokane, Portland and Seattle as their share of the *North Coast Limited* cars operating over their rails from Chicago to Saint Paul and Pasco to Portland, respectively. As a testimony to their sturdy construction, none of these Vista Dome coaches have been scrapped after 49 years, and most are still in active service. After taking over the nation's passenger trains in 1971, Amtrak continued using them for a number of years before putting them up for sale. Here is a list of the cars' present locations:

- 549 and CB&Q 557 are in Spokane, owned by former NP Engineer Mike Gelhaus, who has selected Inland Pacific Rail for his life-long project of restoring a *North Coast Limited* train set.
- 550 is being used by Montana Rockies Rail Tours on its Sandpoint, Idaho, to Livingston, Montana, excursion train. It was one of the feature attractions on a steam special in October 2002 pulled by SP&S 700, which was built to Northern Pacific Class A-3 plans. Northern Pacific Historical Association members, under the leadership of Bill Kuebler, occupied 550.
- 551 is used for Tennessee Central Railway Museum excursions.
- 552 and 553 are owned by Montana Rail Link.
- 554 is running from Williams, Arizona, to the Grand Canyon on the Grand Canyon Railway and has been named "Coconino." I was aboard in May 2002, escorting a Rail Travel Center tour group.
- 555, 556 and SP&S 559 are now owned by the Alaska Railroad.
- CB&Q 558, owned by Tom McOwen, is used on the Indiana and Ohio Railway.

NP 1905 on the Yakima-Cle Elum Local adding new Vista Dome coach 550 to the rear of Train Number 5 at Ellensburg, Washington, July 29, 1954.

The Northern Pacific published route guides for passengers, listing the locations of scenic and historic points of interest along the tracks. The titles of these booklets changed over the years, although the contents remained basically the same. The 1927 edition was called "2000 MILES OF STARTLING BEAUTY!" In 1930 it became "2000 MILES OF SCENIC BEAUTY"; and in the 1940s the title was changed to "SCENIC ROUTE ACROSS AMERICA."

Two pages in the guide books never changed. One began:

> Count the Mountains! See all the Northern Pacific mountains you can on your journey, for they are unsurpassed anywhere in the world! Twenty-eight ranges are visible from your train window—the same vast mountains that Lewis and Clark overcame, rich now in the lore of pioneer days in the Northwest, wearing the mantle of glamour that gold prospector, railroad builder and "dude" rancher have put upon their mighty shoulders! This is the "March of Mountains" as it appears to the watchful westbound Northern Pacific traveler...

It went on to list all 28 mountain ranges in the order of their appearance from east to west.

A companion page was devoted to rivers, prefaced by a summary of the scenery in general: "Pictures all the way—Great Swift Rivers—Forested Shores—Rugged Bluffs—Cataracts—River Birds—Clear Ice-Cold Mountain Streams Plunging from the Woods—Deep Gorges—Bridges."

> For 1,406 miles, two-thirds of the distance between Chicago and Seattle-Tacoma on the North Pacific Coast, the '*North Coast Limited*' of the Northern Pacific Railway travels along the banks of some of the most picturesque rivers in America. It is indeed a route of "scenic beauty." Rivers of Minnesota, fed by 10,000 lakes; rivers of Dakota, through wheat fields and the colorful Bad Lands; rivers of Montana, across vast cattle ranches and into the Rockies; rivers of Idaho, with mountains climbing high overhead; rivers of Washington, which bring life to great orchards; and the Columbia!
>
> After leaving the new Chicago Union Station on the C.B.&Q. the *North Coast Limited* follows the Mississippi River, 'Father of Waters,' for 383 miles; the Historic Yellowstone is followed for 341 miles; the Missoula River, through the most impressive portion of Montana's 'Shining Mountains,' 106 miles; the Clark's Fork from Montana into lofty Idaho Rockies, 93 miles; and the Yakima river, through great, volcanic lava beds and contrasting, blossom-spread valleys in Washington, 141 miles.
>
> Travelers going direct from Spokane to Seattle follow the Columbia River for 7 miles; if they go from Spokane to Portland, the Columbia is followed for 220 miles.

The guide lists 44 additional rivers followed by NP trains.

When four Vista Dome cars were added to each *North Coast Limited* train set in 1954, passengers were given an unexcelled opportunity to see the route's endless scenery. And, to make the viewing perfect, the Northern Pacific implemented dome window-washing facilities at both Livingston and Missoula, Montana.

A specially built rolling ladder stands alongside the westbound *North Coast Limited* at Missoula in June 1955, while the carman cleans the dome glass. Mount Jumbo juts up in the background.

North Coast Limited

In my early Tacoma days, my parents had a unique method of rewarding me for being a good boy. We would climb into our 1927 Model T Ford and first go downtown to the Mecca Restaurant at 13th and Commerce to look at the large cup-of-coffee sign above the entrance. Actual steam wafted upward from this immense cup. From there we proceeded to the old Milwaukee Road depot at 25th and Pacific to witness the *Olympian* departing. I was fascinated by the huge Bi-Polar electric locomotive and its shrill whistle. Last came the highlight of our excursion. Standing alongside Puyallup Avenue not far from the Northern Pacific freight house was an illuminated *North Coast Limited* sign. Somehow, the lighting made it seem like smoke was flowing from the stack of the big Class A engine and there was an illusion that the wheels were turning. It didn't take much to make a small child happy—and for entertainment you couldn't beat the price. It was in the midst of the Great Depression.

My friend Rick Leach recently discovered some old negatives taken by commercial photographer Marvin Boland. Among them was a photo of the *North Coast Limited* billboard that Boland had taken for the C.E. Stevens sign company. Elaine Miller of the Washington State History Museum research center looked up the date in their Boland records—August 26, 1931. I was four and a half years old when this picture was taken.

In August 1943, I made a pilgrimage to Missoula, Montana, to visit the great Northern Pacific photographer, Ronald Nixon. Ron took me out to one of his favorite picture-taking locations near Bonner. He always liked to include block signals, if possible. This was my first opportunity to photograph the *North Coast Limited* at high speed, with a day-coach section moving fast behind NP 2665, a high-wheeling Class A-3 Northern.

The Northern Pacific received its first passenger diesel locomotives in January 1947. (The Lorenz Schrenk/Robert Frey book, *Northern Pacific Diesel Era, 1945–1970,* has a wonderfully detailed chronology of diesel dates.) Before becoming dieselized, the *North Coast Limited* was operated in two sections: one for coaches and the other for Pullman sleepers. They were pulled by NP's magnificent 4-8-4 Northern class steam engines with Class Q-6 Pacifics filling in when needed. One day in 1946, the NP was blocked by a derailment somewhere between Spokane and Easton. The two sections being pulled into Spokane by steam engines were consolidated into one train for detouring over the Milwaukee Road. The relatively new, four-unit, FT freight diesel 6008 drew the assignment of handling this lengthy train. Although it returned to Northern Pacific rails at Easton, 6008 continued on through to Seattle, earning the distinction of being the first NP diesel to pull a passenger train into Seattle.

Unfortunately, I neglected to record the date of this historic event, but I can narrow it down to sometime within a few months in 1946. The photo shows three train order hoops in the rack: one for the engine crew, one for the conductor and head brakeman, and the lowest for the flagman at the rear. The rule requiring orders for the flagman went into effect December, 1, 1945, and passenger diesels took over the *North Coast Limited* in early 1947. That narrows the year down to 1946, and because the man on the platform is in shirtsleeves, my guess is that it was probably in the summer months.

From the end of World War II until late 1952, *North Coast Limited* service experienced the doldrums. New streamlined cars were received, but NP elected to mix them with older, heavyweight cars and keep to the same schedule. In contrast, the Great Northern's *Empire Builder* and Milwaukee's *Olympian-Hiawatha* were completely streamlined, with new, fast running times between Chicago and the Northwest. Here is the semi-streamlined *North Coast Limited* at Mandan, North Dakota, in 1950, where the train was fueled and completely serviced, complete with a windshield cleaning.

A complete reversal in NP's *North Coast Limited* policy came in 1952. Beginning November 16, service was entirely streamlined, with a schedule pared down by 12 hours to match the competition. Once again there was a *North Coast Limited* billboard in Tacoma.

On November 16, 1952, a large crowd at the East Auburn station waits to board the revitalized *North Coast Limited* streamliner for its first dash to Chicago on the new schedule. The train carried its same hallowed name, but had been renumbered from Number 2 to Number 26, the same designation as New York Central's fabled *Twentieth Century Limited.*

The Auburn Roundhouse Drum and Bugle Corps joined the celebration at East Auburn. Most of the instruments were empty oil drums. My good friend, Ed Foisie, was the engineer on this festive first run. When the train arrived in Yakima, Foisie was presented with a large, red delicious apple from Miss Yakima, Marion Stube. A photo of this presentation appeared in the Northern Pacific's *North Coaster* magazine, as did my picture of the Drum and Bugle Corps at East Auburn. All of the passengers on the train were given apples at Yakima.

Wide-open camera views are difficult to find in forested western Washington. At Palmer Junction, 11 miles north of Enumclaw, an entire train is visible as it is about to follow the Green River gorge to Lester in April 1962. It is equipped with Vista Domes, which will enhance the trip over Stampede Pass for the passengers. At the lower right is the 26-mile pipeline carrying water from the Green River to the McMillan Reservoir for the city of Tacoma.

After a fast dash from Seattle to Auburn, it was slow going for the *North Coast Limited* for the next 60 miles. First came the many curves along the Green River and then the steep grade across the Cascades. At Easton, the engineer could widen on the throttle and travel 79 mph for the next 25 miles. Then followed more sharp curves along the Yakima River before reaching Thorp and then the stop at Ellensburg. On April 17, 1965, Number 26 is at Mile Post 13, negotiating a series of sharp curves between Kountze and Dudley. Rumors persisted that the Northern Pacific was going to dig a tunnel there to eliminate the curves. It never happened. The guardrail in the background marks Highway 10, later superceded by Interstate 90.

Darkness obscured some of the Northern Pacific's best scenery along Lake Pend Oreille and the Clark Fork in northern Idaho, but it was daylight in both directions for the *North Coast Limited* over Butte Mountain in the Montana Rockies. This view, taken through a Vista Dome window, shows a profusion of boulders as westbound Number 25 crossed a spectacular curved trestle on June 8, 1955. Such locations underscore how the Rocky Mountains acquired the name.

Westbound Number 25 with Conductor John Hutching and Engineer Charlie Graves is about to make a stop at Bozeman, Montana, on June 7, 1955, after crossing Bozeman Pass and before tackling Homestake Pass and the Continental Divide over Butte Mountain. The Northern Pacific's Bozeman Station starred in the 1992 Robert Redford movie, *A River Runs Through It.*

Northern Pacific rails ended at Saint Paul, Minnesota. From there, Chicago was reached over a subsidiary line of the Chicago, Burlington and Quincy. Here, the *North Coast Limited* Number 25 is making a station stop at LaCrosse, Wisconsin, on August 21, 1969. The "Q" contributed one set of equipment for the train.

Dome coach 558 carries the initials CB&Q at the upper left to show ownership.

The *North Coast Limited* made a rare visit to Tacoma on December 10, 1956, due to a track obstruction on the Stampede Pass line. Westbound Number 25 was detoured over the Spokane, Portland and Seattle Railway from Pasco to Vancouver and then on NP tracks north to Seattle. The SP&S along the Columbia River was a faster route than via Stampede Pass over the Cascades, with fewer curves and no mountains to climb. This resulted in a Seattle arrival that was reasonably close to "on time."

East-West Passenger Trains

North Coast Limited...Alaskan...Mississippi Valley Limited...Pacific Express...Atlantic Express...Twin City Express...Manitoba Limited...Puget Sound Express. These are some of the names that have been applied to various Northern Pacific passenger trains over the years. By the time I hired out in 1943, all NP passenger trains were identified just by numbers, except the *North Coast Limited* and the *Alaskan.* And, only the *North Coast Limited* was considered a "showcase" for the railroad. The *Alaskan* traversed the same transcontinenal route, but had "vintage" equipment and made innumerable stops, some of them lengthy. For example, heading east, the *Alaskan* stopped at Glendive, Montana, for 7 hours 55 minutes, arriving at 1:15 A.M. and departing at 9:10 A.M. in order to comply with a North Dakota law requiring a daytime, local train across the state.

The eastbound *Alaskan,* Number 4, provided day local service across the state of Washington. Its westbound counterpart, Number 3, was a night train, running just ahead of the *North Coast Limited.* No-name Number 5 provided day local service from Spokane, with the same equipment found on Number 4. The older coaches had straight-back, red-and-green plush seats and a café coach (half-diner, half-coach) that provided the usual NP meal service excellence. My favorite car on this train was the reserved seat coach. It had individual, revolving parlor car seats and a modern interior design. Extra fare was required to enjoy this luxury, ranging from 25 cents to one dollar, depending on the distance. It was well worth it, particularly on the western half of the trip, which, among other sights, featured Stampede Pass across Washington's Cascade Range and the gorgeous Green River west of Lester.

In 1952, however, a revolution in Northern Pacific service occurred. The *Alaskan* was discontinued, replaced by the *Mainstreeter,* a new secondary train with far fewer stops than its predecessor, and with the same overall running time as the pre-1952 *North Coast Limited.* It was equipped with lightweight, streamlined cars, as soon as they became available, including the new, popular Holiday Lounge cars.

When the *Alaskan* was discontinued in 1952, day local train Number 6 was established for Seattle to Spokane on the same schedule as former Number 4. These were not trains for those in a hurry, as there could be up to 40 stops between Seattle and Spokane.

Every member of the family appreciates this extra comfort at low cost!

An oasis of comfort for travel between Seattle and Spokane is the air-conditioned, deeply-upholstered reserved seat coach which the Northern Pacific provides daytime travelers on Train 4 eastbound, and Train 5 westbound. A coach ticket (at lowest available fare), plus a small additional charge for a seat, will assure you ease and restfulness.

Reserve a seat for your next trip. Lounge chairs, carpet, streamline interiors and well-equipped dressing rooms, plus air-conditioning, make these coaches even more luxurious than the handsome parlor cars of a few years ago!

Delicious Meals En Route

Club breakfasts in the air-conditioned cafe-coach "next door" cost only 50 cents and up; regular plate meals only 65 cents; table d'hote luncheon 90 cents; table d'hote dinner only $1.00. You can buy sandwiches and beverages for as little as 25 cents an item—and remember, all food is the standard "famously good" Northern Pacific kind.

●

EXAMPLE FARES

One Way and Round Trip Coach Fares and One Way Reserved Seat Fares

AND ☞ BETWEEN ☜	SEATTLE			TACOMA			SPOKANE			YAKIMA		
	One Way	Round Trip	Re-served Seat	One Way	Round Trip	Re-served Seat	One Way	Round Trip	Re-served Seat	One Way	Round Trip	Re-served Seat
Spokane	$6.80	$12.25	$0.50	$6.80	$12.25	$0.50	......	......	......	$3.75	$6.75	$0.25
Cheney	6.80	12.25	.50	6.80	12.25	.50	$0.36	$0.65	$0.25	3.75	6.75	.25
Sprague	6.80	12.25	.50	6.80	12.25	.50	.91	1.65	.25	3.75	6.75	.25
Ritzville	6.80	12.25	.50	6.80	12.25	.50	1.45	2.65	.25	3.75	6.75	.25
Connell	6.25	11.25	.50	6.25	11.25	.50	2.45	4.45	.25	2.75	4.95	.25
Pasco	5.50	9.90	.45	5.45	9.85	.45	3.20	5.80	.25	1.95	3.55	.25
Prosser	4.60	8.30	.35	4.60	8.30	.35	3.75	6.75	.25	1.10	2.00	.25
Mabton	4.35	7.85	.35	4.35	7.85	.35	3.75	6.75	.25	.85	1.55	.25
Toppenish	3.95	7.15	.30	3.95	7.15	.30	3.75	6.75	.25	.43	.80	.25
Wapato	3.80	6.85	.30	3.80	6.85	.30	3.75	6.75	.25	.28	.55	.25
Yakima	3.50	6.30	.25	3.50	6.30	.25	3.75	6.75	.25	......	......	......
Ellensburg	2.75	4.95	.25	2.70	4.90	.25	4.30	7.75	.35	.83	1.50	.25
Cle Elum	2.15	3.90	.25	2.15	3.90	.25	4.85	8.75	.35	1.40	2.55	.25
Auburn	.48	.90 #.77	.25	.43	.80 #.61	.25	6.55	11.80	.50	3.10	5.60	.25

60 day limit unless otherwise indicated. #25 day limit.

I took my first photo of Number 5 in 1941, while returning from a solo trip to Spokane when I was fourteen. The coach I rode in was not air-conditioned and some of the windows were open on this hot summer day, making it possible to lean out for picture-taking. This view was taken in central Washington, somewhere between Pasco and Ellensburg. Behind the tender is a Railway Post Office car, followed by a baggage car, coach, café-coach, and a deluxe Reserved Seat coach. Behind it is an ancient coach with vents along the roof line. It was the brakemen's duty to open the vents for air circulation, using poles with brass hooks on the ends, and to close them before entering tunnels. If brakemen forgot to close them, which happened now and then, passengers were in for a sooty experience.

I enjoyed riding in (and taking pictures from) locomotive cabs, as most of the engineers and firemen were good friends. It also was a fine way to view the territory and gain further understanding, in my role as a dispatcher, about what was happening out on the road. While riding eastbound Number 6 this day in 1953, we were "in the hole" at Pomona (eight miles west of Yakima), meeting Seattle-bound Number 5, behind engine 6507. The westbound block signal arm is just starting to drop as Number 5's engine passes by our cab, while our head brakeman waits to line the switch to put us back on the main track. He is obeying the operating rule requiring him to stand on the side of the track opposite to the switch stand.

This May 1944 photo shows the eastbound *Alaskan,* Number 4, drifting through lonely Wymer station in the Yakima River canyon between Ellensburg and Yakima. I should have been up on the hill on the sunny side of the track for a better view, but the fear of rattlesnakes kept me from straying too far. Number 4 was a convenient train for transferring locomotives to where they were needed. The regular locomotive, a Class Q-6 Pacific-type road engine, is behind Class W-1 Mike 1672, which was on its way to bring back a westbound troop train from Yakima to Fort Lewis. W-1 engines normally were used in freight service, but were fast enough to handle a passenger train if necessary.

Ellensburg was an important stop for NP passenger trains. Up until 1933 it was a division point, with the Pasco Division crews handling trains to the east and Seattle Division crews to the west. During the belt-tightening of the Depression, the Pasco Division was eliminated and the Seattle Division became part of the Tacoma Division, which was extended to Yakima. Under the new arrangement, freight train crews ran through between Auburn and Yakima, but passenger train crews continued changing at Ellensburg. In this photo taken on a cold winter day in February 1948, Number 5 is stopping in Ellensburg for crew change, passengers, mail, and express. My friend, Lyle Lindelien, and I had attempted to drive from Auburn to Pullman for a University of Washington versus Washington State College basketball game, but were turned back by bad road conditions. Lyle's Chevy is parked to the left of the train. My one consolation on an otherwise disappointing day was that I was able to take a few train shots.

Eastbound Number 4 has just descended from Stampede Pass and is about to stop at Easton Station and cut off the four-unit diesel helper. This train has ten cars; five were the most the steam Q-6 road engine could handle over the pass by itself. Each helper crew included a conductor pilot, engineer, and fireman. The conductor pilot is descending the ladder on the front cab, preparing to uncouple the engine. At the lower left is a cinder pit track, where steam engines dumped their cinders. The cinders were shoveled into gondola cars on the adjacent track.

In this scene, westbound Number 5 is making a station stop in downtown Auburn. It was here that I learned a significant lesson about rigid union rules. I had been sent to Auburn to work second trick (4:00 P.M. to midnight). When Number 5 came to a stop, the clerks positioned baggage wagons to unload a substantial amount of mail and express. With a lull in my telegrapher duties, I went out and volunteered to help. One of the clerks brusquely said, "This is clerks' work, go back and tend to your telegraphing." Each craft had a union "schedule" outlining performance duties, which I learned early in my career were rigidly applied.

In this photo, Number 5 is stopped just clear of the Main Street crossing. Today, the old station and NP trains are long gone, but this location still bustles with rail activity. A new *Sounder* commuter train complex now occupies this site. The crossing flagman, too, was replaced long ago with electronic signals.

North-South Coastal Passenger Trains

This shot features Number 407 between Black River and Seattle, 1945. Number 407 and Number 408 could be considered the ancestors of today's *Coast Starlight*. Although these trains did not have names, they were nonetheless spectacular. NP had built and owned the original line from Vancouver, Washington, to Seattle, but in 1910 granted trackage rights to the Great Northern and Union Pacific to share the track. Initially, each road operated as many as four passenger trains each way, some of which were given names. The Northern Pacific, for example, had the *Evergreen State Limited* and the *Portland Express*. Then in 1926, because of dwindling passenger travel, the three roads implemented a pool train agreement. Each road operated one day train each way and

2600
NORTHERN PACIFIC

alternated running the overnight "Owl." Timetables of the three roads showed all of these trains, but did not identify the operating company. Revenue was split evenly, and timetables contained the notice, "Tickets reading N.P., G.N. or U.P.R.R to any point on the joint line Seattle to Portland, inclusive, or on branch lines diverging therefrom, will be honored on any trains on the joint line."

In my early years, the Great Northern ran the morning local from Seattle to Portland and the faster evening schedule, Portland to Seattle. Union Pacific had the morning local from Portland and the evening faster train from Seattle.

Northern Pacific's share in the line were Number 407 (northbound) and 408 (southbound), which had the fastest schedules, stopping only at Tacoma, East Olympia, Centralia, Kelso, Vancouver, and a flag stop at Chehalis. (During the war, Number 408 also stopped on flag at Nisqually to pick up Fort Lewis military personnel.) These two were the most heavily used of the pool trains and normally included:

Two baggage cars
Seven or more coaches
Tavern car
Parlor car with individual revolving seats
Four sleepers to or from California on the Southern Pacific
One sleeper to or from the east on Union Pacific

The so-called tavern car was my favorite, with modernistic, red leather upholstery. It was half lunch counter and half tables for meal service.

My first trip on Number 408 occurred in the summer of 1943. A high school friend had moved from Tacoma to Portland and I went down for a visit. Employee passes were not valid on Numbers 407 and 408, but most NP conductors were good about overlooking this restriction. Number 408 came into Tacoma with standing room only, and consequently a switch engine was sent to the coach yard at Union Station to dig out a couple of standby troop-train sleepers to take care of the overflow. Number 408 departed with 1,200 passengers.

Up until the end of WWII, Number 407 and Number 408 were composed of all heavyweight cars, but as postwar car building progressed they were eventually streamlined. By the time Amtrak took over in 1971, they were all "Loewy green."

Left: I first photographed Number 408 in 1942 before I went to work for the railroad. I was bicycling from Tacoma to Puyallup along Pioneer Way and had packed my Kodak Vigilant folding camera in my bike bag. It somehow seems appropriate that one of my early train photos is of locomotive 2600. It was built in 1926, the year I was born, and was the first of the 4-8-4 Northern types, named after its designer, Northern Pacific. This one was a coal burner, which was unusual for a train serving Portland since Oregon had regulations requiring oil burners to be used in preference to coal.

In 1943 at Tacoma Union Station, Number 407 stopped to unload mail, express, and passengers. Engineer "Red" Bevan had time to inspect the engine and "oil around." During World War II, locomotives on the coast had a shroud over the headlight as a safeguard against potential air raids.

Number 408 thunders across the McCarver Street crossing in Old Tacoma in 1943. Trains leaving town picked up orders "on the fly" here. The engineer grabbed them from a Y-shaped fork with a string looped around the Y and held by a spring clip. Several years earlier, I had performed my first service for the Northern Pacific here at McCarver Street. I just happened to be there on my bicycle when Number 408 went by. The string with the orders broke and they fluttered to the ground. Rules (and the station train order signal) required a train to stop when this happened and go back to fetch the orders. A telegrapher, who noticed me there with my bike, handed me the orders and asked me to ride up to where the train had stopped and deliver them. Little did I know then that most of my working life would be involved in dealing with train orders!

Diesels were coming, but steam engine 2602 was still pulling Number 408 in July 1947 when it roared by Titlow Station near the Tacoma Narrows Bridge. I had been sent there for two weeks to relieve Agent-Telegrapher Nell Bryan while she was on vacation. Number 408's mid-day schedule did not make for ideal lighting conditions, but a Class A engine leaning around the curve at Titlow Station made for a spectacular photo opportunity, regardless of the lighting.

By the mid 1950s, diesel locomotives were assigned to all Northern Pacific passenger trains. Maximum mileage using diesels was achieved with an ingenious arrangement in which diesel consists arriving in Seattle from the east would make a trip to Portland before returning eastward on the *North Coast Limited* or *Mainstreeter.* I remember my friend and fellow dispatcher Don McGregor, however, often saying, "There's many a slip 'twixt the cup and the lip." Now and then a diesel due to set out on Number 408 would be either late in arriving from the east or have mechanical problems. The last of the faithful Class A Northerns, NP 2601, was ready, willing, and able to pinch hit. Here she is on Number 408, crossing the Nisqually River flats, just a few years before succumbing to the scrapper's torch on June 20, 1959.

The highway at left is US 99, later replaced by Interstate 5 in the 1960s.

Diesel power began appearing on Number 407 in 1948. In this photo, almost new unit 6506 is slowing down for the Main Street crossing as it passes Auburn Depot. Now, *Sounder* commuter trains, rapidly growing in popularity, stop at this location. A pedestrian bridge to facilitate movement between the northbound and southbound sides and a large new parking garage are also located here. The old wooden Northern Pacific depot is gone, replaced by elegant shelters for waiting passengers. The once bustling scene of agents, telegraphers, and clerks has been displaced by an electronic machine placidly dispensing tickets.

By the time this photo was taken in 1968, Number 408, consisting of all streamlined equipment, had shrunk in size, principally because so many people preferred driving to Portland on Interstate 5. Today, with frightful freeway congestion, many travelers are returning to the rails and Amtrak's popular *Talgo* trains are running close to capacity.

This scene has changed dramatically since 1990. Tacoma's glorious Union Station is now a Federal Courthouse, and the concourse, depot tracks, and the umbrella sheds were removed to make way for Interstate 705. Amtrak has moved to a new station on Puyallup Avenue.

The near side of the station formerly was occupied by NP's western district accounting office, and the far side was the division superintendent's office and the train dispatcher's office. The employee parking lot shown here now is the location of a new courthouse wing.

Also, a pedestrian bridge to the new Chihuly Museum of Glass extends from the far corner of the station. The Washington State History Museum has been built just beyond the station, and the University of Washington Tacoma Campus is located across the street in renovated historic warehouses. The new Tacoma Art Museum stands to the right of this scene.

In 1952, Number 408 has departed Tacoma Union Station and is passing the Sperry Flour Mill complex. Flour was milled on the right and then moved in sacks to the docks by way of overhead conveyors across the tracks. The mill was closed and the buildings dismantled in 1973 to make way for Schuster Parkway, linking Old Tacoma with downtown. The docks still remain and are home base for the Ready Reserve Fleet of the Military Sealift Command. Ships can be underway after four hours' notice to deliver heavy equipment for military operations anywhere in the world.

NP's first passenger diesel sets, consisting of one cab and two cab-less booster units, were delivered in 1947. This configuration required turning the entire set at the end of a run. Near the end of 1948, the blind unit at one end was replaced with a cab unit, eliminating the need for turning. The first two units of 6504 in this photo were original F-3s and the trailing unit is a newer F-5. The first coach behind the baggage car was one of the original modern, semi-streamlined coaches purchased by NP for the *North Coast Limited* in 1935. It was bumped from that service by postwar lightweight streamlining.

In March 1963, Number 408 emerges from the Ruston Tunnel at the Tacoma Smelter and is about to enter the mile-long Nelson Bennett Tunnel under the north end of Tacoma. The smelter was built in 1890 by W.R. Rust, who sold it in 1905 to the American Smelting and Refining Company (ASARCO). At one time, one-tenth of the nation's copper was refined here. The famous smokestack was built in 1917, rising to a height of 571 feet, making it the tallest in the world at the time. It lost that title in 1937 when nine feet were removed from the top. The smelter was shut down in 1985, partially because of the high cost of pollution controls. The smokestack came down in a spectacular implosion witnessed by thousands on January 17, 1993. None of the buildings in this photo remain today.

The original 1873 NP tracks into Tacoma from the south ran inland from Puget Sound, passing through Rainier, Yelm, Roy, Lakeview, and South Tacoma. Later known as the Prairie Line, it had a steep grade necessitating helper engines for heavy trains. In 1914 NP opened a sea-level route along Puget Sound. The Point Defiance Line, as it was called, connected to the original tracks at Tenino Junction. While the proprietor, NP, used both lines, tenants Union Pacific and Great Northern had to choose one or the other for their trains. The UP elected to use the "Point Line," and GN opted for the Prairie Line to service a considerable number of sawmills along the route. Consequently, GN's passenger trains from Seattle to Portland served Prairie Line towns, while those of the NP and UP did so for the Point Defiance Line. This arrangement continued until 1943, when GN changed to the Point Defiance route for practical and economic reasons. Many of the sawmills were gone and there had been mounting pressure from the city of Tacoma for cessation of the long, heavy GN trains that impeded traffic at the Pacific Avenue crossing.

Consequently, after GN switched to the Point Line, no scheduled passenger trains ran between Lakeview and Tenino Junction. However, an occasionally unexpected event, such as a derailment, landslide, or other track blockage on the Point Line resulted in a detour over the Prairie Line. Such was the case when "Galloping Gertie," the original Tacoma Narrows Bridge, collapsed on November 7, 1940, interrupting normal rail traffic. So did the earthquake of April 13, 1949, which disabled Point Defiance Line bridges.

In this photo, detoured NP Number 408, the midday train to Portland, steams off the 15th Street drawbridge in Tacoma, ready to tackle the Prairie Line's steep grade out of town. The Prairie Line, of course, remained in service for NP local freights.

A class W-3 2-8-2 oil-burning helper engine is giving Number 408 a boost up the 2.2 percent Prairie Line grade; 2.2 percent is known as mountain grade. The little shack on the back of the helper's tender was called the doghouse. It accommodated the head brakeman on freight trains.

Mountain grades were nothing new for 2608, one of NP's original Class A Northern engines designed in 1926 to pull the *North Coast Limited* over the Rockies and Cascades. Here, 2608 has reached the summit of the Prairie Line grade out of Tacoma.

Burlington Northern was in the passenger business for a little over a year—from Merger Day on March 3, 1970, until the birth of Amtrak on May 1, 1971. Service was more or less the same as it had been on the pre-merger roads. NP's *North Coast Limited* and *Mainstreeter* and GN's *Empire Builder* and *Western Star* continued to operate. So did Chicago, Burlington and Quincy's *Denver Zephyr* and *Twin Cities Zephyr*. The *California Zephyr* was reduced to tri-weekly service; ironically, it is the sole survivor of that once-famous fleet, as Amtrak continues the Chicago to Oakland run.

Seattle to Portland service remained the same after the merger, with Burlington Northern providing two round trips per day, and Union Pacific one.

Train 195 in this photo is departing Tacoma Union Station on April 27, 1971, four days before Amtrak took over most of the nation's passenger trains. It is a specter of its predecessor, NP Number 408, which in the heyday of passenger service would have had 16 or 18 cars, including Pullman sleepers bound for California. Looking carefully at BN Number 195, one can trace its ancestry. Lead unit 9828 is former NP 6707A, followed by 9813, which had been NP 6706B. The three stainless steel dome cars deadheading in the train are from CB&Q's *California Zephyr*. Northern Pacific baggage and parlor-bar-lounge cars are next, followed by a Great Northern coach.

After Amtrak took over passenger service in May 1971, the mid-day train from Seattle finally was given a name: *Coast Starlight.* It also provided, for the first time, through service to Los Angeles. The *Coast Starlight* is seen here from the Tacoma Narrows bridge in January 1972, with equipment inherited from various railroads. The lead diesel is a former CB&Q "E" unit from the *Zephyr* fleet, followed by an ex-Great Northern engine. The baggage car and dome care are from the Southern Pacific.

Amtrak was introduced to the Prairie Line on July 2, 1972, when morning Portland train Number 199 was detoured because of a freight train derailment on the Point Defiance line. This photo, again illustrating the mix-and-match nature of early Amtrak consists, shows Number 199 crossing Pacific Avenue in Tacoma. Today, the Burlington Northern-Santa Fe track (formerly Northern Pacific) has been removed to make way for a new downtown light rail line. Access to South Tacoma industries now is via Nisqually, on the other end of the American Lake/Prairie lines.

This is the only photo in my collection that shows my birthplace—the old Saint Joseph's hospital on the skyline just to right of center. A massive new medical center now has replaced the original building.

Northbound "Owl," Number 401, is shown in early morning light departing Tacoma Union Station at 5:25 A.M. on June 22, 1952. Being a quiet Sunday morning in the dispatchers' office, I asked one of my cohorts to watch my desk while I dashed down to trackside with camera and tripod. Photos of the "Owl" are somewhat rare, as there was sufficient light for taking pictures only on the longest days of the year. These were overnight runs between Seattle and Portland, involving an extremely slow seven-hour schedule, departing Seattle and Portland at 11:45 P.M. and arriving at their respective destinations at 6:45 A.M. Numbers 401 and 402 primarily were mail and express trains, but also included coaches and sleepers. One Pullman for each train was set out and picked up at Tacoma, so that Tacoma-boarding passengers could retire before the 1:00 A.M. departure of Number 402 or sleep later than the 5:05 A.M. arrival of Number 401.

Number 401 passing the yard limit sign at Auburn, 5:55 A.M. on June 24, 1952 (my day off). The engineer saw me and waved. My favorite "A" engine, 2602, was doing 70 mph before slowing down for the Auburn Station stop.

NP Branch Lines

Grays Harbor Branch

Nine decades ago, in 1913, 48 passenger trains each day were scheduled at Tacoma Union Station, counting both directions. Twenty-four trains ran between Seattle and Portland; four were Great Northern trains to and from the east; eight made connections with Northern Pacific east-west trains at East Auburn; six served Grays Harbor traffic; and six were Buckley Line trains to and from Kanaskat, one of which made a round trip through to Kerriston. The Buckley Line served Orting, South Prairie, Cascade Junction, Buckley, Enumclaw, and way points. At Cascade Junction, connection could be made with four trains to Burnett and Spiketon, and two trains to Fairfax.

On August 19, 1911, Conductor Perry Hall on train Number 397 from Kerriston to Tacoma sold a hundred tickets to passengers boarding at way points, such as Taylor's Trail, Kangley, Palmer Junction, Bayne, Cumberland, Arline, Crocker, and McMillan. Passengers boarding at the larger towns bought their tickets at the stations. (Perry Hall later was promoted to Rules Examiner and I took my first rules test from him in 1943. He was a fine gentleman and an extremely competent rail, which earned him the honor of being selected as south-end conductor for President Franklin D. Roosevelt's special train in 1942.)

The six passenger trains through Tacoma Union Station that served the Grays Harbor area on the west side of the Olympic Peninsula ran via the Prairie Line to Lakeview, then turned off onto the American Lake Line through Camp Murray and Fort Lewis to Nisqually, and continued on the Point Defiance line for a few miles to Saint Clair. At Saint Clair, trains entered the Grays Harbor branch to go through Olympia, Gate, Elma, Montesano, and Aberdeen to Hoquiam and Moclips.

Until the 1920s, these trains had names. The morning train each way was the *Grays Harbor Limited,* the mid-day train, the *Puget Sound Express,* and the evening run, the *Grays Harbor Express.* The westward *Puget Sound Express* and the eastbound *Grays Harbor Limited* had Moclips for their terminus; the others went to and from Hoquiam.

When I began my railroad career in 1943, the automobile had taken a toll on the railways. Passenger service was long gone from the Buckley Line, the Grays Harbor Line was down to one round-trip daily except Sunday, and there was a mixed train (a coach on the rear of a freight train) from Centralia to South Bend. There were four trains daily each way between Seattle and Portland, and the Northern Pacific continued running shuttle connections from Tacoma to East Auburn to meet east-west trains.

The engineer on the remaining Hoquiam train in the early 1940s was veteran Glenn Portrude, who also was at the throttle of the first train to run on the Point Defiance Line after it opened in 1914. I particularly remember a comment made by Conductor Hostetter during one ride I took on the Hoquiam train. We were moving along at a good clip behind the regular engine, a Class Q-4 Pacific, NP 2187, when Hostetter remarked, "Old Port's got a good swing on them today." It's funny how trivial things can stick in one's memory...

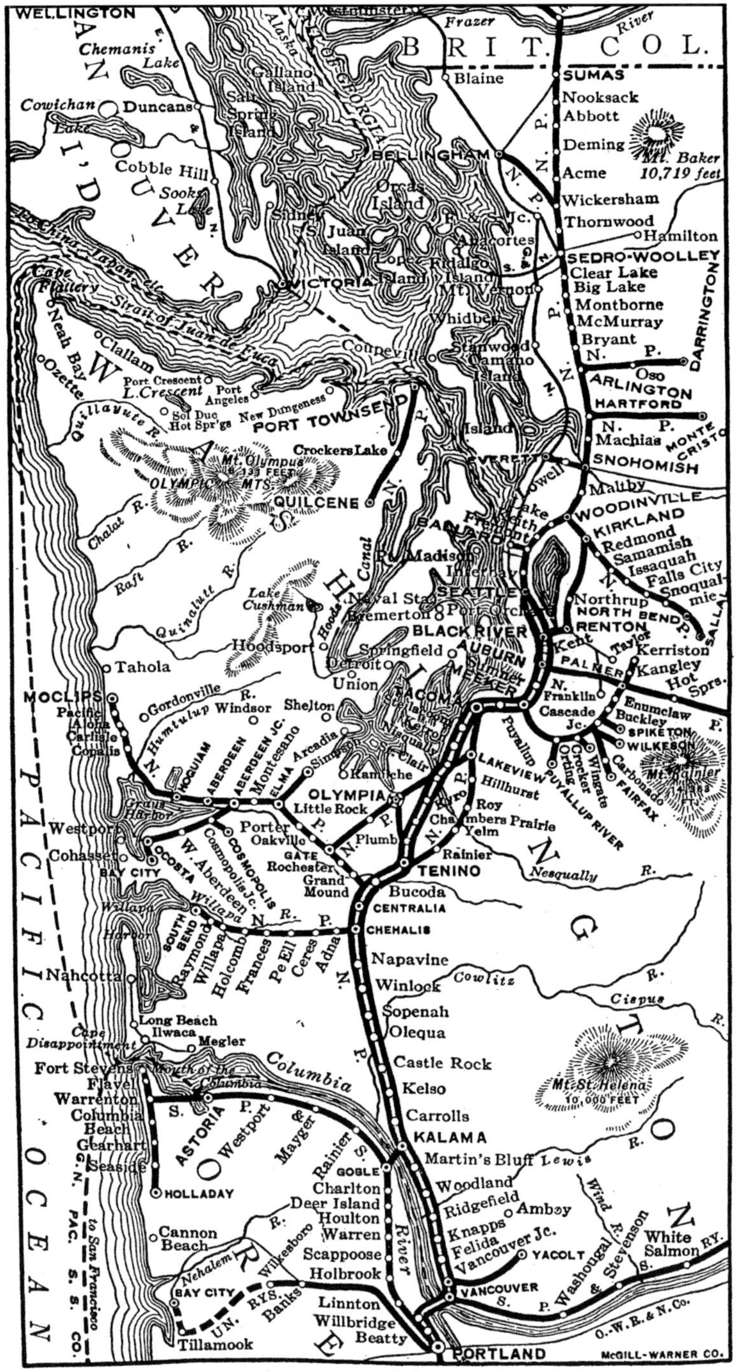

Puget Sound area, showing NP branch lines.

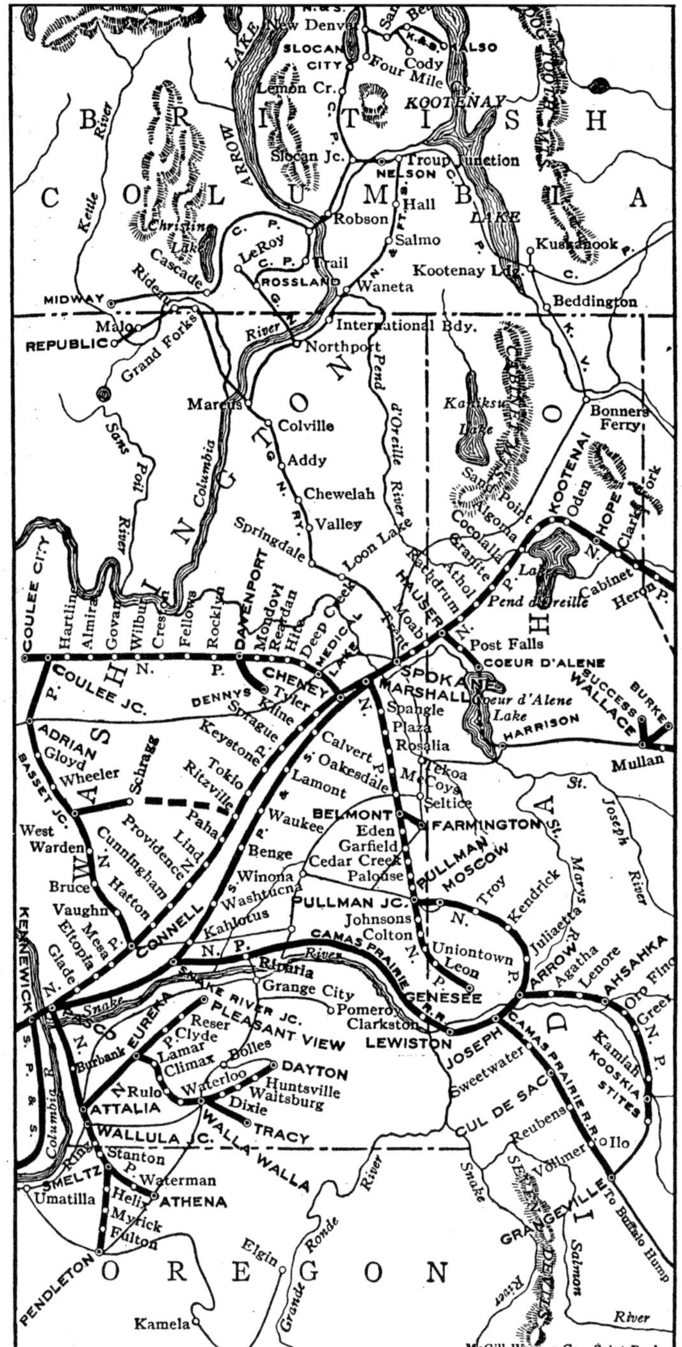

The Inland Empire, showing NP branch lines.

In May 1953, Hoquiam-bound Number 422 comes off the drawbridge over the City Waterway (now Thea Foss) in Tacoma and is about to cross 15th and A Streets before descending to Tacoma Union Station. First behind the engine is the Railway Post Office (RPO) car, which had a clerk to sort mail and exchange mail sacks at stations. There was a slot in the side of the car for people to mail letters; the RPO clerk canceled the stamps. Next is a baggage car, followed by a single day coach, ample for the few passengers then riding the rails on the Grays Harbor branch.

In 1930 the American Locomotive Company delivered a magnificent, new 4-8-4 Northern type locomotive completely equipped with roller bearings, a previously untried concept, to the Timken Roller Bearing Company. Timken had ordered this engine to demonstrate their product to the nation's railways and, over a two-year period, it was tested on fourteen different railroads. The grueling test results were so spectacular that almost all locomotives built thereafter were equipped with roller bearings. The trials were concluded in 1933, after which the Northern Pacific successfully negotiated to purchase the locomotive from Timken. Its original number, TRBX 1111, was changed to NP 2626, and it was assigned to the Tacoma Division. For the next fifteen years, it pulled NP's premier train, the *North Coast Limited,* except on special occasions when withheld for a train of distinct importance, such as Presidential or Board of Directors specials. When diesel engines took over, its use diminished. On May 12, 1953, I captured the low point in the "Timken's" career as it arrived at Auburn station pulling the humble Seattle to Hoquiam train Number 422. The regular Class Q-6 Pacific type engine assigned to this run had experienced mechanical problems in Tacoma on the return from Hoquiam the night before. A freight engine had been substituted to finish the run to Seattle. The next day, 2626 took Number 422 from Seattle to Tacoma, where the repaired Q-6 was restored to its usual assignment.

The Hoquiam passenger train's last run came on February 18, 1956. Here, the Seattle to Hoquiam train sits at the Olympia station, four days before its final trip. The Railway Post Office car previously had been discontinued and the consist is pared down to a baggage car and coach. Conductor Frank Hodges and Engineer Frank Willmott visit with the Olympia switch crew while an operator works the express.

The same lonesome train awaits its 2:55 P.M. departure from Hoquiam to Olympia, Tacoma, and Seattle on a dismal February 14, 1956. The only passenger train now using the station, it will be gone in four days. In 1914, this was known as Hoquiam Union Station and bustled with activity. Oregon-Washington Railroad and Navigation Company and the Chicago, Milwaukee and Saint Paul each had four arrivals and departures, while the Northern Pacific listed sixteen. In addition to the Seattle trains, there was service to Moclips, McLeary, Cosmopolis, Markham, Ocosta, and Bay City.

Willapa Harbor Branch

In my early years with the Northern Pacific, passenger service continued on the Willapa Harbor branch line to Pe Ell, Raymond, and South Bend, although reduced to a mixed train. For many years there had been two daily passenger trains to South Bend: one from Centralia, and, up until 1930, one running through from Tacoma. The evening train was called the *South Bend Limited.* In the 1930s steam consists were replaced by gas-electric motor cars, which in turn were discontinued in the early 1940s. In their place, a combination baggage-coach car was added to the rear of the South Bend freight run, making it a mixed train.

Here, Engineer Bill Raymond leans out the window of gas-electric B-18 on the stub track at Centralia Station, ca. 1935, waiting for departure to South Bend. At this time there was a Northern Pacific restaurant on the north side of the depot, which was a three-building complex. At the south end was the express office, and in the center, the telegraph office, ticket office, and waiting room. B-18 included a Railway Post Office compartment behind the engine room, space for baggage, and a passenger section at the rear. When the *South Bend Flyer* became a mixed train, B-18 was used for several years in Montana, ending up on the Oakes to Staples run.

Combination coach 1195—behind a box car on the South Bend mixed train—stands ready for passengers to board at Centralia in March 1954, one week before its final run. At the time, no one appreciated this historic piece of equipment; it was considered "ancient" in a negative light. Northern Pacific historian Lorenz Schrenk, in a vast research project, compiled a comprehensive list and history of all NP passenger cars from 1870 to 1970, including the story of coach 1195. It was built by Pullman in 1901 for the Saint Paul and Duluth Railroad, and became NP first-class coach 840 after NP purchased the Saint Paul and Duluth. In 1922, it was upgraded at the Pullman shops to a steel underframe smoking car and renumbered 1181. Later it was made into a dormitory-smoker, and finally, in 1938, converted to a baggage smoker and assigned number 1195.

I recall two outstanding features of car 1195 in particular: ornate brass lamp fixtures from the gaslight days, and beautiful stained glass in the arches above the windows. It was retired at the Como shops in 1956 and scrapped. I wish it had been saved.

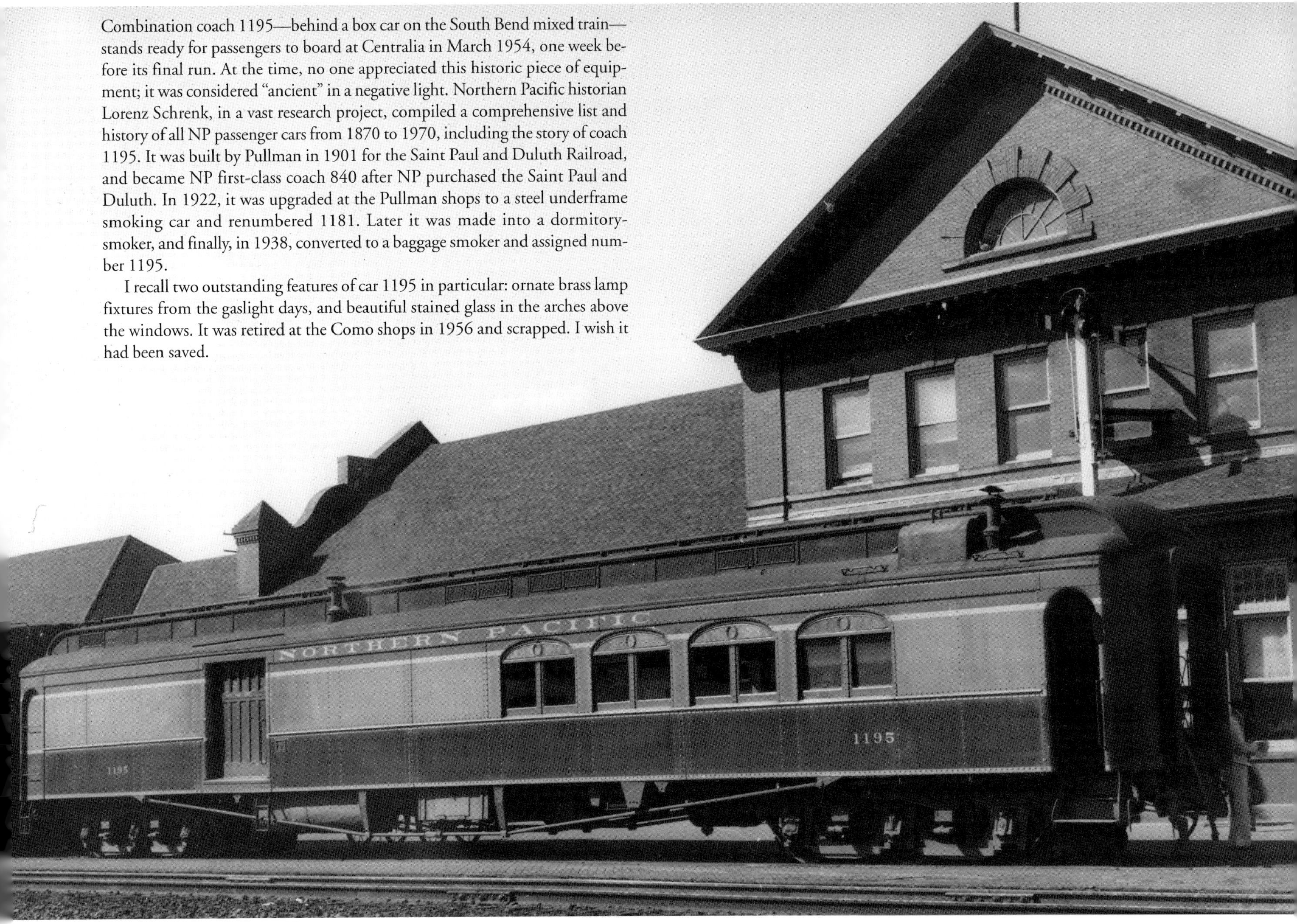

The South Bend mixed train used a short, five-mile segment of the busy Seattle- Portland double track main line from Centralia to Chehalis Junction. Then it took a sharp right turn on to the 57-mile long branch to Willapa Harbor and the twin towns, Raymond and South Bend. A short distance down the branch, a highway overpass made it possible for me to take a photo showing the entire train with its assortment of freight cars ahead of combination coach 1195. Albert Farrow and I "chased" it all the way to South Bend, since it would be our last chance to photograph a mixed train in our part of the country. A few days later on March 15, 1954, I rode on the last run of this mixed train.

Pe Ell, the midway metropolis along the South Bend branch, once was a busy logging and lumbering center. I caught the branch's mixed and freight trains meeting here.

Pe Ell stands at the bottom of a 1.4 percent grade up Pluvius Hill. Westbound steam engines needed a full tank of water before commencing the climb.

Frances is located at the bottom of the hill to the west of Pluvius. Again, there was a water tank—although not the usual Northern Pacific wooden style. The mixer that day, with enough water to make it to the next tank at Raymond, highballed through Frances at full speed. One of the old nicknames for the NP passenger train on this route in its heyday was the *South Bend Flyer.*

The train divested itself of freight cars here at Raymond, and continued on to the end of the line at South Bend with only the combination coach. Eventually, the Willapa Harbor branch was abandoned and the rails removed. Today, a portion is designated as Willapa Hills Trail State Park and is maintained for hiking and biking. A trailhead at Pe Ell has an interpretive sign displaying some of my photos and artifacts.

Palouse and Lewiston Branch

During the 1920s, the NP began replacing steam-powered trains operating on branch lines with self propelled, gas-electric coaches in an attempt to trim losses on these runs. A steam train with locomotive, baggage cars, and coaches required an engineer, fireman, conductor, and two brakemen. The gas electrics included everything in one car—Railway Post Office, baggage, and coach space—and required only the services of an engineer and conductor. In keeping with the money-saving theme, these were no-frills cars, and the seats were not designed for comfort. The light rail on branch lines contributed to a bumpy ride with lots of rocking and rolling. For that reason they earned the nicknames, "galloping goose" and "doodlebug." An old joke on the Bellingham branch begins with a comment made by a passenger to Conductor Ed Jensen, "The ride seems a lot smoother today." To which, Ed replied, "That's because we jumped the track and have been riding on the ties."

In January 1955, NP introduced a major upgrade for passengers on the P&L, the Palouse and Lewiston branch. A new rail-diesel car (RDC), B-30, was purchased from the Budd Company for the Spokane to Lewiston run. These RDCs had luxurious interiors and were much faster and quieter than the galloping-goose types. The exteriors consisted of stainless steel with fluted sides and were similar in appearance to cars on the famous Budd-built *Zephyr* trains operated on the Chicago, Burlington and Quincy. B-30 served the Inland Empire until February 28, 1966, when it was replaced by Greyhound bus service.

B-30 left Spokane in the morning and returned from Lewiston in the afternoon. I have often wondered if patronage might have been better if the P&L train had departed from Lewiston in the morning, so people in the outlying areas could spend a day in Spokane before returning to Lewiston in the evening.

My wife, Cereta, grew up in St. Maries, Idaho, about 30 miles east of Northern Pacific's P&L Line. A few months after B-30 arrived on the scene, we had a splendid opportunity to see and photograph this new wonder while visiting Cereta's sister, Gabrielle, and her husband, Sully Sullivan. With my two sons, Jim and Tim, and Sully with his children, Robin and Brad, we drove to Oakesdale, Washington, on the morning of June 12, 1955. Sully and the kids boarded the B-30 and I chased it in the car, taking pictures all the way from Belmont, Washington, to Moscow, Idaho. This is typical Palouse country, with rolling hills and wheat fields, but not a lot of people to patronize passenger trains.

NORTHERN PACIFIC

Above: Between Palouse and Pullman, B-30 passes over a lonely country road. This is a rare, peaceful scene in this day of congested freeways.

Opposite: Train Number 311, B-30, crossing the Palouse River between Garfield and Palouse. In the early 1950s, I had been submitting photos to *Trains* magazine, with no success. Finally, I sent this photo with a note saying, "I refuse to give up." Back came a check and a note from Editor David P. Morgan, "You don't have to give up." The B-30 on the bridge appeared in the October 1955 issue of *Trains*. Incidentally, this issue carried a story headlined, "The Great RDC Race," about three Budd cars coupled together that made a rail-fan run from Washington, D.C., to Chicago in the incredible time of 12 hours and 29 minutes, a full hour faster than any previous run. The 214 passengers and crew declared they never enjoyed a train ride so much or felt less travel fatigue.

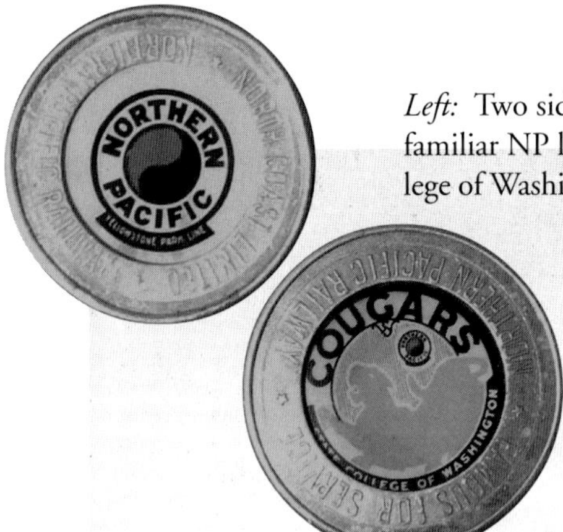

Left: Two sides of a Northern Pacific metal paperweight. One side bears the familiar NP logo. The other side is inscribed with "Cougars" and "State College of Washington," along with a graphic of the college's mascot.

Number 311 made its major stop in Washington at Pullman, home of Washington State University. Over the years, thousands of students from all over the Pacific Northwest passed through this classic station on their way to or from college. A 1935 Northern Pacific brochure tells what the railroad had to offer:

> Northern Pacific special train service for the opening of Washington State College has become an institution. It performs the important function of providing returning students with the opportunity for renewing old friendships and making new acquaintances before becoming associated in the class rooms.
>
> The Cougar Specials are popular. They are an accepted part of the College. Only Washington State College faculty members and students are allowed as passengers. Chaperones are provided and friends may arrange to be in the same car. All sorts of fun for everybody!
>
> These specials are fine trains in every respect. Pullmans are comfortable, dining cars serve those "famously good" meals and an observation car provides all of the other modern travel conveniences.
>
> You will enjoy the trip back to college. You will like the friendly atmosphere and the courteous, efficient service of the train crew.

The brochure also cites the cost of a year's attendance at the college: $450 dollars for tuition, room and board in a dormitory, and all fees. If a student wished to live in a private home, room and board costs for a month ranged from $18 to $35!

Shortly after leaving Pullman, B-30 scoots across the state line to travel in Idaho for the remainder of the trip to Lewiston.

Train Wrecks

Clearing House for Trouble

For operations supervision the NP was divided, as were other railroads, into divisions. Although there were eventual changes, when I arrived on the scene in 1943 there were seven, each with a headquarters city:

Lake Superior—Duluth, Minnesota
St. Paul—Minneapolis, Minnesota
Fargo—Fargo, North Dakota
Yellowstone—Glendive, Montana
Rocky Mountain—Missoula, Montana
Idaho—Spokane, Washington
Tacoma—Tacoma, Washington

Each headquarters accommodated a superintendent and his staff—trainmaster, roadmaster, master mechanic, bridge and building supervisor, and chief dispatcher. The chief dispatcher's office was open 24 hours a day, 7 days a week, and served as the nerve center of the division. Mickey Reiersgard, a conductor adept at wood carving, once brought a heart-shaped plaque into the Tacoma dispatcher's office. He had carved on it, "Heart of the Division." Those words certainly rang true.

The division was divided into dispatching districts, each under the watchful eye of a "trick" dispatcher, who had direct supervision over the movement of trains in his territory. Each shift also had an assistant chief dispatcher, who supervised the trick dispatchers and was responsible for the general operation of trains. Ensuring that locomotives were available for all trains, and that crews were in place for unscheduled trains, were fundamental duties of the dispatchers. Coping with unexpected events made the job of being a dispatcher fascinating to me. I became a trick dispatcher on June 15, 1949, started extra relief work as assistant chief in 1964, and became night chief dispatcher in Tacoma in 1969. On this assignment, I came to work at midnight and relieved afternoon chief, John Ackley, son of the chief dispatcher who had hired me as call boy in 1943. John had one of the best descriptions for our office that I ever heard: "Clearing house for trouble."

When a problem arose on the division it was usual practice to call the dispatcher's office for a solution, particularly at night when the higher officials were home in bed. Most of the calls were relatively minor, involving fairly easy solutions, but now and then we received the dreaded call from a conductor or engineer: "We are all over the ground!" A train was off the track! Our initial challenge was to make all of the necessary phone calls fast enough; the division superintendent, trainmaster, roadmaster, road foreman of engines, and nearest section foreman all had to be contacted, along with claim agents and railroad police. If a wrecker was needed, we made those arrangements, too. Then we focused on how to handle the other trains that could not proceed on the affected track. If the line would be out of service for an extended period of time, efforts were made to reroute trains on adjoining railroads or on circuitous branch lines. If detours were made on "foreign" roads, we arranged for pilots to accompany the detoured trains (pilots were conductors and engineers serving to guide train crews over unfamiliar territory). Conversely, there were times when the other roads—Great Northern, Milwaukee, and Union Pacific—needed to detour over Northern Pacific lines and we would provide pilots for them. When the electrified Milwaukee needed to detour over our line, steam engines had to be made available to pull their trains.

After a derailment, I often visited the scene to make a photographic record, sometimes at the company's request. Wrecks grew to be a significant part of my railroad photo collection.

Jim Fredrickson, taking the "trick room" picture at right. Photographed by Dispatcher Don McGregor.

"Trick room"—Northern Pacific's Tacoma Division dispatchers' office at Tacoma Union Station in 1943. The division was divided into dispatching districts, with each dispatcher governing movement and issuing the train orders for his territory. Left to right: Andy Kelly, Point Line, Tacoma to Centralia; William "Bucky" Walters, Mountain West, Auburn to Easton; Maynard Hanson, Double Track South, Centralia to Vancouver; Fred Bradbury, Branches (this job had only Morse telegraph communication to the wayside operators; all other desks were connected to their stations via railroad telephone lines); and Earl Newman (top of head showing on right behind shelves), Mountain East, Easton to Yakima. Sitting out of sight at far right, Frank Ryan, Double Track North, Tacoma to Seattle. A few years after this photo was taken the office was remodeled, and each dispatcher was provided with a semi-secluded cubicle allowing for better workplace concentration.

Collision at Auburn Yard, August 24, 1944
Switch Engine 1268, First 679, and Second 680

I had worked for the Northern Pacific a little over a year before seeing my first train wreck. It happened on the double track main line at Auburn Yard on August 24, 1944, and it was a bad one, although fortunately there were no fatalities. Switch engine 1268 collided with freight train First 679 on the northbound track, pushing locomotive 1777 over onto the side of freight train Second 680 on the southbound track. A switch had been incorrectly lined.

Art McKay, engineer of switch engine 1268, was seriously injured. Engineer Charlie Hoffman and Fireman George Ballard of the 1777 were scalded and bruised. Kenny Doxon, brakeman on First 679, and Jack Shoemaker, fireman on the 1268, suffered bruises.

Northern Pacific operated two fast overnight freights from Portland to Seattle, First 679 and Second 679. A sizeable portion of First 679's cargo was fruit and vegetables in refrigerator cars from California received from the Southern Pacific at Portland and destined for Canada. These cars were set out at Auburn and switched promptly to the ice house for re-icing in time to continue on Train Number 675 later the same morning, bound for Canadian connections at Sumas.

For many years, Class W-3 2-8-2 locomotives, NP's sturdy "workhorse," were the usual power on the 679s. During the final years of steam, Class A 4-8-4 Northerns also were used, when available.

This unfortunate event ended the 42-year career of switch engine 1268, a 2-8-0 Consolidation type. It had been built by the American Locomotive Company, Richmond Works, in 1902, and was deemed not worth the expense of repairs. It was dismantled at South Tacoma on March 6, 1945.

NP employees taking stock of switch engine 1268 and freight engine 1777 at Auburn Yard, August 24, 1944.

Right: Badly damaged Class W-3 engine 1777, a 2-8-2 Mike, sandwiched between switch engine 1268 and cars on train Second 680. The locomotive was sent to the South Tacoma shops, underwent a $20,000 repair job, and was pulling trains again in three months.

Below: Reconstructed 1777 at the same location, 3½ years later on February 10, 1948.

Rear End Collision at Quendall, Washington, April 22, 1952

On April 22, 1952, I must have been sheltered by a hand of fate. At the time I was working as third trick dispatcher for Double Track North, which covered the double track from Tacoma to Seattle and all of NP's north end branches. It was my day off, but I wanted to make a trip over part of my territory and had elected to go for a ride on the Everett-Auburn Turn from Everett through Snohomish, Woodinville, Kirkland, Black River, and on to Auburn. I left Tacoma at 11:05 A.M. on Union Pacific passenger train Number 457 for Seattle, where I boarded Great Northern's *International* Number 360. I got off that Vancouver-bound train in Everett at 2:25 P.M. and then hiked across town to the NP yard office. It was customary to ride the engine on "student trips" to get the best possible view of the territory. However, the train was just departing as I arrived, so I had to settle for catching the caboose. No problem, I thought. I would move up to the engine when we stopped to pick up cars at Snohomish. But, abnormally, there was no pick-up at Snohomish that time. So, instead, I thought, I'll get on the engine at Woodinville. But, as we arrived there I was in the midst of a lengthy conversation with Conductor Elroy Westby, and, first thing I knew, it was time to depart and I was obliged to remain on the caboose. It seems as though some invisible force was keeping me off the engine. Our next stop was sudden and severe; we ran into the rear end of the "Woolley" local, which was switching at Quendall, four miles north of Renton. At the formal investigation held in the trainmaster's office at Auburn a few days later, the engineer described what happened to the engine at the moment of impact.

Assistant Superintendent Ernie Price, conducting the investigation, asked: "When the collision seemed imminent, what was done by all these people [engineer, fireman, head brakeman, swing brakeman] in the engine cab?"

Engineer: "Well, I opened the door on the left side and walked out to the front end and stood on the step until I was about ten feet from the caboose we were going to hit, then I let go."

Price: "Did all these others get off?"

Engineer: "As to that I couldn't say—it was everybody for himself."

Everyone did get off without injury. Actually, I was the only one to shed any blood. When we suddenly stopped, my head was part way out of the cupola window of the caboose and I struck the window frame. I still have a small scar above my left eye as a souvenir.

Assistant Master Mechanic Charlie Moreau described the damage:

> The caboose which was struck rode up over the drawbar and took off the forward portion of the superstructure or nose of this diesel back to the cab pushing the cab up over the roof of the engine damaging all of the control stands, brake valves and everything in the cab.

Fortunately, no one was in the Woolley Local's caboose at the time.

I have always wondered what the outcome might have been had I succeeded in getting to the head end. Would I have been the one who didn't get off?

After reviewing the investigation, the company decided it was the result of improper flagging in non-block signal territory.

GP-7 diesel unit 558 only had been in service one month before wrecking at Quendall.

Demolished engine 558 cab, where I had planned to be riding.

Two views of the wrecked wooden caboose of the Sedro Woolley-Auburn Local. Fortunately, none of the crew were inside—they were on the ground doing switching duties.

The "Big Hook," Auburn wrecker Number 41, prepares to lift wrecked diesel engine 558 back on the track at Quendall. This was before hard hats became mandatory at work sites.

South Tacoma shop workers performed their usual stellar restoration job on GP-7 diesel unit 558, and she returned to service three months after the Quendall wreck. I always admired the ability of the South Tacoma shop workers to take in apparently "totaled" locomotives and turn them out looking like new.

Derailment of GN First 671 near Steilacoom, June 7, 1952

The whisky bottles in these boxes were empty, being sent to Canada to be refilled. Railroad policemen were on hand to assist spectators in resisting the temptation to help themselves to products in the wreckage.

$500,000 GREAT NORTHERN TRAIN WRECK GIVES TOWN OF STEILACOOM A FIVE-DAY ROMAN HOLIDAY.

Worst spill on Point Defiance line since it was opened in 1914 draws huge crowds to site of fantastic 31-car pile up.

This was the headline in the Friday, June 13, 1952, edition of the newspaper, *Lakewood Log.*

The Northern Pacific owned the double track line between Seattle and Vancouver, Washington, but shared it with the Great Northern and Union Pacific, which had "trackage rights" for operation of their trains. NP maintained the line and also took charge of clearing derailments when they occurred.

At 2:25 P.M., June 7, Great Northern hot-shot freight First 671, pulled by three-unit diesel engine 309, left Vancouver heading north with 90 loaded cars, one empty car, and a caboose. Charlie Bond was the engineer and with him in the cab were Fireman Stu Parks and Head Brakeman Ernie Searle. Swing Brakeman Mel West rode in the rear unit. Conductor Cole Ellis and Brakeman Bob Childers occupied the caboose. A 15-minute inspection stop was made at Centralia and Operator Lee Elliott gave them a roll-by inspection at Nisqually, reporting them passing the station at 6:15 P.M. No defects were noted. About ten minutes later, there was a loud noise on the dispatcher's telephone and communication was lost. First 671, traveling 50 mph, had crossed Bridge 16 about one mile from Steilacoom when the emergency air brakes were activitated and the train came to a sudden, jarring stop and wrecked. The engine was about 200 yards from the Steilacoom Depot. Brakemen, who went out in both directions to flag approaching trains, saw that they had been in a monumental derailment. Thirty-one cars were derailed and compressed into a space of 534 feet, making what the *Lakewood Log* called "a gigantic pile of junk." None of the crew was injured, although the two men in the caboose received a severe jolt. A hobo riding on one of the freight cars suffered a crushed leg and was taken by ambulance to a hospital.

Railroad claim agents had their hands full coping with the damaged lading. Included in the mess were Folgers coffee, potatoes, California onions, gypsum, furniture (including a crated piano), margarine, coal, powdered glue, cases of empty Seagram's whisky bottles, and three carloads of new Fords. Railroad police (also known as yard bulls, cinder dicks, and gum shoes in railroad lingo) assisted in detering looting and keeping onlookers at a safe distance.

The Point Defiance line was out of service for four days until enough cars were removed to allow the laying of a temporary bypass. In the meantime, all trains were rerouted via the South Tacoma, Lakeview, Fort Lewis line.

The usual formal investigation to determine the cause and affix responsibility was held five days later at Tacoma Union Station in the NP superintendent's office. Normally, an investigation was conducted by an official at the trainmaster level or perhaps by an assistant superintendent. But because of the staggering cost of this derailment and the huge claims to be settled, the heavy hitters were brought in. Superintendent Tom Kane conducted the investigation, backed up by Assistant General Manager Caleb Corser from Seattle. Great Northern officials present included Superintendent Ira E. Clary.

No one involved was charged with a rules violation. Great Northern was quick to point out that there had been a sun kink on Bridge 16 a week before the derailment, but it had been repaired by the Steilacoom section crew. Engineer Bond said that he had observed a slight bend in the rail at this location, but was afraid to make an emergency brake application because passenger train Number 458 was due. He said there had been no noticeable roughness going over this rail. GN bridge men who were present at the inquiry intimated that the bridge may not have been properly repaired from the previous sun kink. NP countered by pointing out that the derailment commenced after the train had passed over the bridge and the cause must have been something breaking on a car, such as a wheel or axle. At the time of the investigation, there still was considerable debris to sift through at the crash site. The exact cause was not pinpointed.

First 671 had derailed onto the Puget Sound shoreline. At high tide, the box car on the left, filled with automobile parts, was almost submerged.

NP's biggest Tacoma Division wrecker, Number 41, based at Auburn, was sent all over the division for major jobs. A smaller Tacoma wrecker worked at the other end of the derailment.

In a fast-moving derailment, cars often jackknife and climb atop one another.

GN's First 671 three-unit diesel locomotive, jackknifed and crossways to main track.

Rear-end Collision near Steilacoom, NP First 679 and GN First 671, July 8, 1952

Disaster again struck the busy Point Defiance Line one month later at 11:35 P.M., July 8, 1952, at Ketron, about two miles south of Steilacoom—this time with fatal results. Leading a parade of trains was Northern Pacific Number 693, the "Highball" from Hoquiam, which stopped to pick up cars at Pioneer Sand and Gravel, just north of Steilacoom. Following on its heels was NP Seattle to Portland fast freight First 679, with Great Northern's First 671 not far behind. First 679 stopped briefly behind Number 693, while 693 finished its pickup. Dave Lewis, the flagman of First 679, threw off a lighted fusee (warning flare) before they stopped, then dropped off the caboose to go back and flag. In the meanwhile, veteran Conductor Fred "Sambo" Sampson remained in the caboose cupola. Dave was only about twenty feet behind the caboose when his engineer sounded a proceed signal. Before returning to the caboose, as an additional warning to the following train, he placed two explosive "torpedoes" on the track, which would produce a loud bang when run over by an engine wheel. Just after boarding the caboose, he saw GN First 671 fast approaching. Lewis shouted a warning to Conductor Sampson and jumped off. Tragically, "Sambo" was unable to move from the cupola to the back platform quickly enough and was fatally injured. He was a 39-year veteran with Northern Pacific and highly regarded by all who knew him. It was a stunning loss.

First 671 had been moving 54 mph as it approached a block signal showing a yellow indication, which required speed to be reduced sufficiently to stop at the next signal. The next signal was red, because NP First 679 was stopped ahead. At that point, GN First 671 applied the emergency brakes, but it was too late to keep from striking First 679's caboose at 28 mph.

The NP wooden caboose was reduced to kindling. Sturdy, steel cabooses began appearing on the NP about ten years after this wreck. Now cabooses have virtually disappeared, and all crew members ride in the engine.

Rear-end Collision involving NP Local and GN First 672, Winlock, September 8, 1952

Northern Pacific's Centralia to Vancouver Local had the assignment of switching at the various communities along the way—Napavine, Winlock, Vader, Castle Rock, etc. At Winlock, September 8, 1952, Conductor Marty O'Toole and engineer George Waring, along with the fireman and head brakeman, were placing some cars on the house track. Rear brakeman Al Merryman remained on the caboose. At 2:45 P.M., Great Northern freight First 672, with three-unit diesel engine 307, approached from behind. Both trains were using the northbound track, as the southbound was out of service for repairs, which meant there was no block signal protection. Although rules required trains to proceed through Winlock slow enough to stop for any obstruction, First 672 was moving a little too fast. When Merryman noticed that First 672 could not stop in time, he jumped off the caboose and ran. The engineer, fireman, and head brakeman all jumped off First 672's engine 307, too. No one was injured. The Great Northern engineer's first comment was, "This engine is a 'Jonah.'" It was the same locomotive that two months earlier had run into NP First 679 at Steilacoom.

Great Northern locomotive 307 nudged the NP caboose off the track before demolishing four empty log flatcars.

NP caboose 1249 was knocked off its trucks (wheels) and turned completely around before coming to rest alongside the right-of-way.

Northern Pacific officials were on hand to supervise the rerailing and clearing of rubble from the track.

Number 675 Derailed at Acme, Washington, October 5, 1952

Northern Pacific operated a daily through freight from the big classification yard at Auburn, Washington, to Sumas on the Canadian border. Cars bound for Canada arriving at Auburn on transcontinental freights Number 601 and 603, as well as traffic from the south coming in on trains 679 and 685, all proceeded north on Number 675, a very important train. At Sumas, the cars were turned over to the Canadian Pacific and the British Columbia Electric Railway for movement to final Canadian destinations.

In this case, heavy rainstorms had blocked up water from a culvert under the track at Acme, Washington, 24 miles south of the border, washing out the roadbed. With no automatic block signals on this line to give warning to Number 675 of trouble ahead, a derailment occurred.

After getting off work at the Tacoma dispatchers' office at 8:00 A.M., I traveled to the scene of the wreck, accompanied by my fellow night shift dispatchers, Don McGregor and Don Shane.

Dispatchers extraordinaire Don McGregor and Don Shane (hands on locomotive), endeavoring to push the derailed engine upright. Or maybe they were preventing it from falling further…?

Four-unit NP 5408 off the track at Acme. Track Department and Mechanical Department crews worked together to rerail the train and repair the track.

Freight Train Derailment at Thorp, Washington, November 11, 1953

Overheated friction journal bearings, or "hot boxes," were a major problem for many years on railroads. Loss of lubrication at the end of an axle caused overheating to a point that the weight of a car could break off the weakened steel. All cars built since 1963 are required to have roller bearings. This, plus the installation of trackside heat detectors, have virtually eliminated derailments due to hot boxes.

On November 11, 1953, my good friends Conductor Merle Routt and Engineer Tom Mathews were following *Mainstreeter* Number 1 from Yakima at 3:10 A.M. on a westbound freight with 73 cars. It was foggy in spots up the Yakima River canyon, but they and brakemen Joe Doros, Bill Schmidt, and Bill McKean could keep a fairly good eye on their train as it rounded the many curves. They passed Ellensburg at 4:20 A.M., planning to stop at the Bristol siding to let *North Coast Limited* Number 25 pass by. As Tom looked back on a curve coming into Thorp, he noticed a red, fuzzy glow. Setting the air brakes, he radioed Merle, "I think we have a hot one, better head in on the siding at Thorp." However, they didn't quite make it to the siding before the journal failed and the axle dropped. They were traveling at 35 mph when the train derailed.

Journal failure at the end of an axle that caused Thorp derailment.

An axle end on a good set of wheels.

Night Chief Dispatcher Don McGregor and a Northern Pacific official assessing the damage at Thorp. Conductor Merle Routt commented that, throughout his 37 years with the railroad, he had "never seen so many cars in such a short space."

Fortunately, the badly damaged tank cars did not contain flammable or hazardous materials.

Cases of Del Monte canned goods spilled from an overturned box car.

Steilacoom Bridge Fire, March 28, 1954

This was the setting at the Northern Pacific Dispatchers' Office, Tacoma Union Station, 5:20 A.M., Sunday, March 28, 1954—In the "trick room" were Jack Darragh on the Double Track North (Tacoma to Seattle and north branches), Don Shane on the Double Track South (Tacoma to Vancouver and South Bend branch), and Jim Fredrickson, working the Mountain (Auburn to Yakima plus the Grays Harbor and Bremerton branches). Next door in the chief's office were Night Chief Dispatcher Art Overman and Crew Caller Virginia Handy.

Sunday mornings normally were quiet, with no locals running and no train lineups to issue, as the track workers enjoyed a day off. But on this Sunday morning, Art burst out of his office into the trick room, shouting "Stop all trains!" Initially, we thought he meant all three of us, but soon enough we realized that his directive was aimed at Don. The guards at the McNeill Island Federal Penitentiary had spotted a railroad bridge on fire across the water and immediately called the railroad. The warning came just a few minutes too late, as Union Pacific northbound freight Number 691 already was on the bridge. The "F-27" Report of Accident gives a graphic description of what happened:

> Between Ketron and Steilacoom 515AM Train UP 691 Conductor Reese Engine UP 1561 (Lead unit) Engineer Boyce with 83 cars, 16 damaged.
>
> Fire and Derailment. Train rounded curve and was on Bridge 15.1, a 513-foot, 33-bent trestle before learned center section was on fire. Engine and 26 head cars crossed when 27th to 38th cars inclusive (12 cars) became derailed and caught fire. In addition the four rear cars of the 26-car cut on the head end became derailed. The 12 cars afire or in water and expected to be a total loss are: four cars loaded with merchandise, one with wax, one with candy, one with shoes, one with rugs, one with cloth, two with refrigerators and one with ore. [The report gives each car number.]
>
> Will be necessary to replace a 300-foot section of this bridge before can open eastward [southbound] main track. Meantime will be necessary to detour via 4th and 17th Subdivisions [via South Tacoma and Fort Lewis]. Expect open eastward about March 30th.
>
> Combined efforts of one Foss tug, one Coast Guard fireboat and Tacoma City fire truck with two fire lines required to extinguish fire which was accomplished about 845 AM.
>
> Injured: L.R. Pearson, Union Pacific brakeman of Portland, particle in eye. Will lose no time.

It was a costly disaster, but fortunately there were no serious injuries. As soon as I went off work at 8:00 A.M., I was on my way with a camera.

One of the Coast Guard's "Matchbox Fleet" battles the fire on the bridge at Steilacoom.

Cutter CG-83527 has the blaze under control.

Above: Two pile drivers at work rebuilding the destroyed bridge sections. NP crews did almost all of the road's bridge and track work.
Below: Auburn wrecker 41 (left) and Tacoma wrecker 21 lift a Union Pacific box car body onto a flatcar.

4th of July Wreck at Renton, 1955

The words "4th of July wreck" bring sad memories to most NP veterans in the Puget Sound area. It was such a tragedy! NP served Everett with the Auburn to Everett and Everett to Auburn Time Freight. Normally, the diesel crew left Auburn shortly after midnight to run via the Lake Washington Belt Line on the east side of Lake Washington, arriving in Everett before 8:00 A.M. They would lay over all day and come back that evening. However, on July 4, 1955, because of the holiday, they were allowed to "double back" without the usual layover.

Meanwhile, Transfer Crew 2, based out of Auburn, spent the day switching Kent-Renton area industries with engine 1373. They were moving backwards in Renton when they collided with the early train from Everett. The diesel crew suffered minor injuries, but it was a different story for those on the steam engine. Engineer Welborn C. Armstrong was killed almost instantly. He was 72 years old and a 51-year NP veteran. Fireman John Severson, scalded by steam, remain trapped in the twisted cab. Two doctors came aboard and amputated his legs while welders with torches cut away the steel pinning him down. Their efforts were futile; he died 10 minutes before being moved from the cab. He was 27 years old, and a Korean war veteran. His brother, Dallas "Tex" Severson, was an NP brakeman and conductor for many years.

Above: On this 4th of July holiday more than a thousand spectators gathered to watch the wrecking crane tug on 1373.

Left: NP GP-9 diesel units 218 and 219 of the Everett to Auburn Time Freight had been received from the Electro-Motive Division of General Motors less than a month before colliding with the Renton switcher. This proved to be the end of 52 years of faithful service for 1373, which was built by the Baldwin Locomotive Works in 1902. She was scrapped at South Tacoma in the following October.

Rear-end Collision at Centralia, NP First 680 and UP 692, August 5, 1955

Just before midnight on August 4, 1955, two hot-shot Seattle-to-Portland freight trains, Union Pacific Number 692 and Northern Pacific First 680, were ready to leave Tacoma. Number 692 made it to the UP Junction switch in downtown Tacoma first and departed in the lead. After stopping in East Olympia to pick up cars, Number 692 continued on to its next pickup at Centralia. This is where NP First 680 failed to stop and crashed into the rear end of Number 692. Fortunately, the UP crew had got off the caboose. Considerable damage was sustained by the cars of both trains, and the fireman and head brakeman of NP First 680 sustained minor injuries. The outcome could have been much worse.

Demolished freight cars under the Marian Street viaduct at Centralia, smashed into by NP diesel units 6700ABC on train First 680, visible on the right.

Cupola and roof of Number 692's caboose alongside NP engine 6700B and C.

Rear unit 6700C of NP First 680 with cupola and roof of Union Pacific caboose on the left. The head brakeman riding in this unit was cut by flying glass.

Trailing units 6700BC on First 680, showing jackknifed cars of its train. The steam engine at top center is shoving the wrecker train into position for rerailing cars and engines.

Rose Bowl Wreck—Puyallup, December 29, 1960

At the time of this derailment, Northern Pacific, Great Northern, and Union Pacific still participated in a "pool" agreement for passenger service between Seattle and Portland. Each road ran one train during the day and they alternated on a yearly basis for the midnight "Owl." Revenue was pooled and divided among the three roads. Great Northern had the morning run, Union Pacific the evening one, and Northern Pacific the mid-day train. Northern Pacific's Number 408 carried the heaviest passenger load, since it made a direct connection with Southern Pacific's *Cascade,* which ran from Portland to Oakland, California. Passengers bound for southern California then transferred to the *San Joaquin Daylight* at Martinez.

On December 29, 1960, 450 passengers crowded aboard Number 408 at Seattle's King Street Station. Many of them, including Minneapolis Mayor Ken Peterson, were on their way to the Rose Bowl to witness the University of Washington Huskies battle Minnesota's Golden Gophers. It was a festive atmosphere, although a number of the coaches on the train were relics pressed into service for the busy holiday season. Unfortunately, there was an obstacle ahead. Though this was a double track line, a freight train derailment at Puyallup had taken the southbound track out of service. Number 408 received orders at Auburn to back over onto the northbound track at Sumner (NP did not believe in facing point crossovers) and take it to Meeker at the eastern edge of Puyallup. At Meeker they were to switch on to still another track, called the Third Main, to pass around the derailment, then cross back to the southbound main track at the far end of Puyallup. When Number 408 reached Meeker, the engineer apparently forgot about the orders to go on to the Third Main and passed over the 15 mph switch at 49 mph. The engine's three units rolled over, while the cars behind continued on for a short distance before the emergency brake application stopped them. It was a sad case of a veteran engineer, with many years of outstanding service, having a brief mental lapse. The incident marked the end of his career; he retired on the spot.

Thankfully, injuries were relatively minor to passengers and employees. Eighteen were taken to nearby hospitals; five were admitted and the others treated and released. An elderly passenger was quoted as saying, "We've got God to thank it wasn't worse."

A major concern for many of the passengers was getting to the Rose Bowl in time for the football game. A substitute train quickly was made up in Seattle and sent to Puyallup to pick up the eight cars that had not derailed, and the train was on its way again, five hours late. Southern Pacific held the *Cascade* at Portland to connect.

Lead unit 6700C was one of the engines earning the "hoodoo" label. Five years earlier it had been involved in the rear-end collision at Centralia, when NP First 680 ran into UP 692. Two years after the Rose Bowl incident, it was destroyed in a tragic derailment of the *North Coast Limited* at Granite Lake, Idaho.

Two cars, coaches 1346 and 1365, jackknifed and skidded across Pioneer Avenue, seven others derailed, and eight remained on the rails. Fortunately, no automobiles were struck on the busy avenue.

Number 408's three-unit engine consisted of 6700C-6512B-6507C. When the diesel units rolled over, the passenger cars behind continued down the track for a short distance.

Unique Photo Opportunities

Sperry Mill Implosion July 2, 1973

For many years, the Sperry Mill Division of General Mills was a major Tacoma industry. Carloads of wheat rolled in by rail on a spur line above the mill complex. Milled flour was poured into large sacks, many of which were conveyed to a dock across the main line tracks and loaded onto ships for export. My father, Martin Fredrickson, was a longshoreman. I remember him coming home exhausted after long shifts packing 150-pound sacks of flour on his shoulder to stow in the hold of a vessel. (The reason that the sacks were so heavy was because the Panama Canal charged according to the number of sacks onboard; it was advantageous to the shippers to boost sack weight while keeping the overall tally down.) Sperry Mill ceased operating in 1965. The old waterfront automobile road from downtown Tacoma to Old Town passed under the Sperry Mill through a one-lane tunnel. The Sperry Mill removal was part of a 1970s project to replace this old road with four-lane Schuster Parkway. X-Demex Corporation of Dublin, California, was selected to destroy the concrete tower. Burlington Northern's Tacoma Terminal Manager, Milt Whitsell, arranged for me to photograph the event. I was delighted with this assignment, in part because it permitted me to get beyond the restraining line set up for the general public. X-Demex did a perfect job imploding the tower; no debris at all fell on the track. (Apparently the company liked my photos, because I received a number of repeat orders.)

The implosion occurred after Amtrak Number 14, the *Coast Starlight,* had passed. All rail traffic was held up until the demolition was completed.

The concrete Sperry Mill tower just before the implosion.

The explosive charges have been fired, and for a split second Sperry Mill imitated the leaning Tower of Pisa.

A giant dust plume arose as the tower hit the ground.

With dust still lingering, BN Number 147, bound for Portland, was the first train to pass after the blast.

"Top of the Ocean" Fire, April 3, 1977

Early Sunday morning, April 3, 1977, after opening the front door of our north-end Tacoma home to bring in the paper, I spied a large cloud of smoke in the direction of Old Town, about a mile away. I grabbed my camera and headed toward the plume. It turned out that "Top of the Ocean," one of our favorite restaurants, was engulfed in flames. By the time the first fire engines arrived, thick, black smoke gushed from every vent. The initial alarm came in at 6:55 A.M., and the fire was declared under control two hours and 11 minutes later at 9:06 A.M. The flames gutted the "Top" from one end to the other.

It had been built for $100,000 in 1946, but an estimate to rebuild it in 1977 came to $3 million. Though the restaurant was insured, its ownership could by no means cover that amount. The "Top of the Ocean" faded into fine-dining memory.

In the mid 1940s, shipbuilders had been hired to construct a restaurant structure resembling a ship, fitting for this Commencement Bay location. Tacomans enjoyed teasing visitors, saying the "Top of the Ocean" was an old boat that had crossed the waters of Puget Sound before finding a resting place on Ruston Way. Opening June 15, 1946, the "Top of the Ocean" was one of Tacoma's grandest restaurants, with seating for 700 people, as well as three private dining rooms. A bar was added when liquor by the drink was permitted three years later. There were private clubrooms on the second floor, and comfortable offices, living quarters, and a private bar on the third deck. It was popular for banquets, and some of my early dispatcher friends held their retirement dinners there, among them Fred Bradbury, "Abe" Emmons, and my first boss, Chief Dispatcher Austin Ackley.

The fire was the result of an incredulous act of arson. The arsonist hired a taxi to take him to the restaurant. Instructing the driver to wait, he entered the restaurant with cans of paint thinner and ignited a fire. He was captured a short time later, and convicted at a trial in the following June.

The "Top of the Ocean" has been rebuilt—in model railroad HO scale. It is one of the highlights of the train exhibit being installed by Puget Sound Model Railroad Engineers at the Washington State History Museum in downtown Tacoma.

In 1976, Burlington Northern train Number 139 passes by the popular "Top of the Ocean" restaurant across from the McCarver Street station in Old Town. Though a year since the merger, the two trailing locomotive units retain their original colors: 724 had been Northern Pacific 6012A, and 4261 was Spokane, Portland and Seattle 323.

(Above) Though responding quickly, the Tacoma Fire Department found a raging inferno already engulfing the restaurant. Fire fighting equipment, including a fire boat, put out the stubborn blaze *(right)*.

With the fire under control, train traffic resumed. Here, Burlington Northern Train Number 148 approaches the McCarver Street crossing.

Special Trains

There was a time when special trains provided variety and spice to the routine operations of a railroad. Events drawing multitudes of people needed additional passenger trains to accommodate the crowds, particularly when regularly scheduled trains had insufficient capacity. Delegates to conventions of large fraternal organizations such as the Shriners, Elks, Eagles, Moose, etc., often traveled by chartered trains, usually with all-Pullman sleepers. In 1964 I rode in a special train from Tacoma to the National Boy Scout Jamboree in Valley Forge, Pennsylvania. Though it consisted of all pre-war, heavyweight Pullman sleepers, I never experienced better accommodations on a train.

The special train causing the most excitement and intense preparation was POTUS—President of the United States. When I arrived on the scene in April 1943, dispatchers still were talking about President Franklin D. Roosevelt's Northwest inspection tour on the Northern Pacific during the previous November. A pilot train ran twenty minutes ahead of the President's Special to ensure the track was safe and free from sabotage. At night, telegraphers had been called on duty at stations that normally were closed. When the train stopped to take on water, armed soldiers stood by as guards. The nation was quite jittery at this early stage of the war.

Division superintendents rode the president's train over their divisions, as did road foremen, trainmasters, and carmen. Bridge and building supervisors inspected all bridges and tunnels, and section foreman did the same for switches and track in the daylight before the train passed. And, of course, the president's train and the pilot train had priority over all other trains. Furthermore, it was supposed to have been kept secret that FDR was aboard. However, when a secret service agent was seen walking a Scotty dog on the station platform during a service stop at Billings, Montana, people recognized the president's well known pet, Fala.

This 1903 photo of President Theodore Roosevelt's train parked by a Northern Pacific water tank was copied from a postcard owned by my close friend and fellow dispatcher, Raymond C. "Smitty" Smith. Smitty started as a telegrapher in 1923.

When President Theodore Roosevelt visited western Washington in May 1903, it was a kinder and gentler time. A Columbia River bridge at Vancouver had yet to be built; consequently, TR's special from Portland went up the south side of the Columbia to Goble, Oregon, and was ferried across to Kalama, Washington. For twenty-four years, this was the method for moving trains across the Columbia. The photo shows TR speaking to a crowd at Kalama shortly after the train was pulled off the ferry. Roosevelt was welcomed to the state by Governor McBride. The *Tacoma Daily Ledger* reported the trip in great detail, including the following humorous incident:

> The engine that pushed the president's train on to the ferry boat *Tacoma,* on which it crossed the Columbia River from Oregon, had a live bear cub attached to a pole on the tender. The president was greatly interested in the little fellow and, boarding the engine, patted its head. The bear failed to appreciate the honor and signified his disapproval by uttering baby bear growls.

After leaving Kalama, the next stop was Chehalis, where Roosevelt spoke from the McKinley stump. This stump had been cut from a giant tree near Pe Ell and brought to Chehalis in 1901 to serve as a podium for President William McKinley. For many years it remained in a small park between the Chehalis NP station and freight house. It has since been moved to a park on the east side of town.

The "Ferdinand Magellan"

Until late 1942, presidents rode in standard, private Pullman cars when traveling by train. A specific car was not designated for this duty, although the *Roald Amundson* frequently was assigned, as was the case with President Roosevelt's 1942 trip to the Pacific Northwest. In early 1942, just after the United States entered World War II, White House aids Michael Reilly and Steven Early suggested that the president should have a custom-built railroad car to afford maximum protection when traveling by rail. FDR approved of the idea after being told that the car would be used not only for him, but by future presidents as well. The *Ferdinand Magellan* was selected and withdrawn from general service, and sent to the Pullman Company's Calumet Shops near Chicago for complete rebuilding.

President Roosevelt's only request for the design was to "make it a little more comfortable." The interior of the car was redesigned. The number of bedrooms was reduced from five to four, allowing more space for the dining room and observation lounge. Nickel-steel armor plate, 5/8" thick, was riveted on the sides, floor, roof, and ends of the car. Three-inch-thick, bullet-resistant glass was installed and sealed into the window frames, replacing conventional safety glass. Two escape hatches were built into the car, and special trucks, wheels, and roller bearings were installed to support the additional weight, which increased from 80 tons to 142.5 tons, making it the heaviest rail passenger car in the United States.

FDR traveled an impressive 50,000 miles in the *Ferdinand Magellan* during his presidency, but President Harry S Truman was destined to use the car more than any other president. Roosevelt preferred to travel at 35 mph, because it was more comfortable for his paralyzed legs with their braces. In contrast, Truman liked to go fast—80 mph. During his famous whistle-stop campaign in 1948, he logged more than 28,000 miles and made 350 speeches from the rear platform. I took this photo of the *Ferdinand Magellan* as Truman's train left Auburn on June 11, 1948, but, unfortunately, he was not aboard. His next stop after Tacoma was Portland, but the tracks were under flood waters north of Vancouver. Consequently, Truman traveled by auto, while the train detoured over Stampede Pass to Pasco, and thence to Portland. This picture was taken into the sun, so the detail is not very good, but it is possible to compare the changes since President Theodore Roosevelt's time. The Great Seal of the President of the United States can be seen on the rear platform and public-address loudspeakers are mounted on the roof.

The *Ferdinand Magellan* was declared government surplus in 1958. In 1985, however, it was declared a National Historic Landmark by the U.S. government, the only passenger railcar ever to be so honored. It now is on public display at the Gold Coast Railroad Museum in Miami, Florida.

The Turbo Train

Over the years, attempts were made to design faster, more efficient and comfortable passenger trains. These new trains were sent around the country on demonstration tours.

One of my earliest train recollections dates back to 1934. I would accompany my father to the longshoremen's hiring hall, which at that time stood a few doors down from the Spar Tavern in Old Town Tacoma. While he conducted business I would go to the back window in hopes of seeing a train. On one particular day, a train like I had never seen before flashed by, looking like a streak of yellow. It was the Union Pacific's first of many streamlined trains, which toured the country from Washington, D.C., to the West Coast, including a visit to the Chicago Century of Progress Exposition. It made a stop at Tacoma Union Station for public inspection. After the tour, it was assigned to the Kansas City-Salina run and named the *City of Salina.*

In 1947 came General Motors *Train of Tomorrow,* exhibiting Vista Dome cars and letting the public see how much more luxurious streamlined cars were than the old pre-war heavyweights. After the tour, UP purchased the train and used the cars on its Portland to Seattle pool train.

Another General Motors concept came to the Northwest in 1956, the Aerotrain. Two demonstrator sets were built, but the cars were flimsy and uncomfortable. They finally found a home on the Rock Island in commuter service but were scrapped after a few years.

United Aircraft Corporation got into the act in 1968 when it designed and built Turbo trains, conceived on aerodynamic principles and powered by aircraft-type gas turbine engines. They were marketed by Surface Transportation Systems, Sikorsky Aircraft Divison, and participated in the U.S. Department of Transportation's Northeast Corridor high speed ground transportation project between New York City and Boston. Canadian National ordered five Turbo Trains for the Montreal-Toronto service later taken over by VIA.

In 1971 the Department of Transportation and Amtrak sent one of these trains on an exhibition tour to the West Coast. It was received from the Southern Pacific at Portland on August 28 and made a brief stop at Tacoma, where I boarded the train accompanied by my daughter Kim and her friend, Cathy Higgins. In this photo taken at King Street Station in Seattle, the girls are standing under the words Turbo on the power car, Kim on the right, Cathy to the left.

Kim Fredrickson and Senator Warren G. Magnuson at King Street Station, Seattle, after arrival of the Turbo Train on August 28, 1971. The senator was an ardent supporter of passenger rail service.

Magnuson Special Amtrak Train, July 13, 1980

In his last campaign for the U.S. Senate, Warren G. Magnuson chartered an Amtrak special to run from Seattle to Pasco on July 13, 1980, via Burlington Northern over Stampede Pass. It was pulled by an Amtrak F40 PH locomotive and made up as follows: one 84-seat Amfleet coach; one 54-seat Amcafe car; one 84-seat Amfleet coach; and private car Illinois Central Gulf 28 "JoViLa" with observation platform on the rear for addressing crowds.

Stops for passengers and speeches were scheduled at East Auburn, Ellensburg, Yakima, Toppenish, and Pasco. The train departed Seattle at 9:00 A.M. and returned at midnight.

During my teenage years and to this day, one of my best friends has been John M. Coffee, Jr., whose father was a Democratic congressman from Washington's 6th District. Congressman Coffee served in Congress when my idol, FDR, was president. He also was a good friend of Washington senators Magnuson and Henry Jackson. Therefore, I wanted to be sure to get a good photo of Senator Magnuson's campaign train. Where better than at the viaduct

east of Lester? It was a "one shot only" opportunity, as there would be no chance of catching up with the Amtrak special—the rough Stampede Pass forest service road was not made for train chasing.

Haile Selassie Special Train, June 1954

The King of Kings, Conquering Lion of the Tribe of Judah and Elect of God rode aboard this train in June 1954. These were titles borne by Emperor Haile Selassie of Ethiopia, who was on a two-month long, 7,000 mile tour of North America. He had been highly regarded in the United States since Mussolini's fascist troops invaded his country in 1935–36. President Franklin D. Roosevelt invited the emperor to visit the United States when the two met near Cairo after the Yalta Conference in 1945, but Selassie was unable to come at that time. President Dwight Eisenhower invited Selassie again in 1954 and this time he was able to accept. The Emperor and his entourage were feted at major cities throughout the U.S. and Canada. He addressed a joint session of Congress, the United Nations, and the Canadian Parliament. His visit to the Pacific Northwest included a tour of Grand Coulee Dam. In this photo, Selassie's special train is passing through Tacoma along Dock Street. The industries in the background now are all gone, replaced by condominiums, the Chihuly Glass Museum, and the Thea Foss Waterway development. The NP General Manager's private car at the rear of the train accommodated the Emperor.

The Bicentennial Train, April 30, 1976

In 1974, Southern Pacific Daylight engine 4449 was selected to pull the American Bicentennial Train. It would tour the country with 26 cars, displaying over 500 precious treasures of Americana, including the Declaration of Independence, the United States Constitution, the original Louisiana Purchase, Judy Garland's dress from the *Wizard of Oz,* Joe Frazier's boxing trunks, and even a rock from the moon. Consequently, 4449 was moved from Oaks Park in Portland, where it had been on display, to Burlington Northern's Hoyt Street roundhouse for restoration under the direction of Doyle McCormack. After it was returned to working order, and painted red, white and blue, it departed Portland on June 20, 1975, for Chicago, where it met the train.

The special train included twelve baggage cars outfitted with moving walkways along the exhibits on display. In 1975 and 1976, seven million people visited the train during its tour of all 48 contiguous states. It was on exhibition at Seattle, and at North Fort Lewis for Tacoma-area visitors. I pulled off at an overpass near Snohomish on April 30, 1976, and, incidentally, hit upon a unique location for photographing a train carrying the Declaration of Independence—Mile Post 1776.

Amtrak Special Train, June 27, 1971

Amtrak was in its infancy when operating this special train on June 27, 1971, for a rail fan trip, Portland to Tacoma and return. When northbound, it ran over the Prairie Line from Tenino Junction to Tacoma, and I chased it with my camera over this segment. Now I'm glad I did. The track from Tenino Junction to Yelm has been torn up, and just recently the rails were removed from this Pacific Avenue crossing in Tacoma to make way for the new light rail line from Freight House Square on 25th Street to downtown. Seen here behind former Spokane, Portland and Seattle diesel units 805 and 806 is a Great Northern heater car and four former GN coaches. Chicago, Burlington and Quincy Vista Dome observation lounge *Silver Lookout* brings up the rear. Unfortunately, NP was not represented in the train; however, the special is running on former NP track.

The "Gratitude Train"

This photo, taken at Olympia in 1949, represents a special movement rather than a special train. France was devastated during World War II. In 1947, two years after the war ended, millions were going to bed hungry. *Washington Post* political columnist and radio commentator Drew Pearson suggested that well-fed Americans do something to help our former ally. He came up with the idea of sending a boxcar filled with food to France and got the ball rolling by donating $1,000 of his own money. His plan met with instant approval and donations poured in from every state in the Union. The end result was 700 boxcars filled with tons of food, clothing, and medical supplies, which were loaded onto the S.S. *American Leader* in New York City. The name of the vessel was changed to *Friend Ship* for the voyage to LeHavre, France, just before Christmas.

The French responded with a wonderful and ingenious "Thank you." Fifty thousand gifts were collected, some expensive and others simple drawings by children with the words, "Thank you for the food," scrawled on the bottom. A suggestion by a French railroad worker solved the problem of how to deliver the gifts to the individual states and the District of Columbia. During World War I, several hundred box cars that had been built in France between 1852–85 for shipping freight, horses, and cattle were pressed into service to carry troops, including American soldiers, to the front lines. Notice the French words at the top of the center door—"*Hommes 40, Chevaux 8.*" Translated, this means "Men 40, Horses 8," from which is derived their historic name "*40 et 8*" ("40 and 8") cars. Forty-nine of the cars were located, repaired, painted, and filled with gifts for each of the then 48 states, plus Washington, D.C.

In the U.S., the little box cars were transferred to flat cars for movement to each state. The Northern Pacific moved Washington's car to Olympia without charge by billing it as an "empty car," even though it carried 1,001 items. The conductor of this train from Yakima to Auburn was L.M. Blanchette, who had been a sergeant in the 338th Field Artillery in France during World War I. He commented, "The cars were supposed to hold 40 men or eight horses, but they forgot about barracks bags. We used to be jammed in. Had to stand." The "*40 et 8*" sometimes confuses people into thinking both men and horses were carried. According to Blanchette, there was hardly room for one *or* the other!

In Olympia, Governor Arthur B. Langlie accepted the car from French representatives. Originally, it was decorated with forty-four colorful shields, each representing a French province. By the time I took this photo, these had been removed, leaving a number showing their location. Today, the car is well preserved and kept at Sarg Hubbard Park in Yakima.

Stampede Pass

Northern Pacific labeled itself "First of the Northern Transcontinentals," which was indeed a proud accomplishment. First, the Rocky Mountains were conquered and then, several years later, the equally difficult Cascade Range.

When the gold spike was driven in Montana in 1883, western moving Northern Pacific trains went down the south bank of the Columbia River to Portland on Oregon Railway and Navigation Company track. After 1884, NP built to Goble, Oregon, and crossed the Columbia on a ferry to Kalama to connect with NP tracks to Tacoma. The ultimate goal, however, was to construct across the Cascades to Puget Sound. After NP surveyors explored several proposed routes over the rugged range, they narrowed the choices down to three—Snoqualmie, Stampede, and Naches passes. Seattle agitated for Snoqualmie Pass, which would direct the rails toward that city. Yakima and Tacoma favored Naches Pass. The decision was left primarily to NP Principal Assistant Engineer Virgil G. Bogue, who in 1884 recommended Stampede Pass, which he himself had discovered in 1881. He reasoned that this line would traverse the entire Yakima Valley, including the most fertile portions of Kittitas County, and it was the easiest route to Tacoma, which had been selected as the western terminus.

Four years before, on December 27, 1880, Bogue had reported to Northern Pacific headquarters in Tacoma, where he was instructed to assemble a survey party, follow the Green River to its headwaters, and locate a pass for the railroad through the Cascade barrier. This was an absolutely miserable assignment in mid-winter, but data on snow depths was a high priority. For the next three months, Bogue and his party battled first drenching rain, then heavy snow—all the while cutting their way through heavy underbrush and forest. Finally their efforts paid off, as described by Bogue in a report to the American Geographical Society:

> Starting early on March 19th, with our route for the morning at least settled upon, and with favoring skies that lighted our hearts, we made excellent progress. A little after nine o'clock appeared a sharp bend in the ridge to the north, as anticipated. We descended along a well-defined crest so rapidly that in less than an hour the barometer marked only 3,495 feet elevation at a point where for a little distance about us there were no trees. It was evidently one of the lowest points on the divide. To the east a spur cut off much of our view but facing west we looked down on Sunday Creek. Beyond its confluence with the Green were the mountains to the south, covered with dark fir forests, and back of them the great snowy mass of Mount Rainier sharply defined against the blue sky. It was a beautiful scene, so impressive that for a moment all were silent. Thence we continued our trip northward, finding several other depressions in the range but none as promising as the one just described.

Bogue named the location Pass Number 1, hoping it might be named for him in honor of the discovery. Instead, NP officials called it Garfield Pass, after the recently assassinated president. That moniker, however, did not stick. A few weeks after the pass was named, Bogue became dissatisfied with his men's progress in cutting trails. As they were camped by a small lake near the pass, Bogue brought in a new foreman, a notorious "slave driver," in an attempt to force harder work. The men rebelled, gathered up their bedrolls, and took off for Tacoma. Only one of them, Johnny Bradley, remained behind. When a replacement crew arrived, they found a board he had nailed to a tree, christening the place "Stampede Camp." Soon the lake was bearing the name, and then the pass. It has been Stampede Pass ever since. Later, NP renamed the lake as Monad Lake, after its Yin Yang trademark, but locals preferred calling it Lizard Lake.

The new line would include a two-mile tunnel at the summit. Northern Pacific advertised for sealed bids, receiving twelve, which were opened on January 21, 1886. The winner was Nelson Bennett, whose costs were close to half of those submitted by some of the others. The railroad had imposed a requirement that the job be finished in 28 months or the bidder forfeit $100,000 plus 10 percent of the contract price. This provision, plus the immense difficulty that would be encountered in hauling equipment and material to the site, were the reasons for the higher bids. Bennett already had built 250 miles of Northern Pacific track in Montana and had the contract to build from Pasco to Ellensburg. He knew the NP survey engineers personally and had confidence in meeting their 28-month time estimate. When newspaper writer and Tacoma promoter George Francis Train heard of the tunnel contract award, he sent Bennett a telegram reading "Bore, Bennett, Bore! Bore, Bennett, Bore!"

Before boring commenced, a great amount of machinery, men, and equipment had to be moved to the work site. Included were two small locomotives, the *Ceta* and *Sadie,* named after Nelson Bennett's two young daughters. Northern Pacific track had been completed only as far as Yakima, 82 miles away. From there, transportation was dependent on wagons and sleds. The first wagons left

Nelson Bennett's locomotive, *Ceta,* shown with cars hauling diggings from the tunnel. They tilted for dumping, as seen at the rear of the little train.

Yakima on February 1—only eleven days after the contract was signed. When approaching the mountains, the wagons sank up to their axles in mud and melting snow, making it necessary to build a moving roadway of planks. Then they encountered deep snow, fierce winds, and rivers to cross. The project required a strength of will that is difficult to comprehend. Nelson Bennett and his brother, Captain Sidney Bennett, through sheer force of character, kept the men working, although there was a large turnover at first. Sidney, who was superintendent of the project, wrote to his brother, saying he kept three teams of workers busy, "One coming, one drilling, one quitting." Work commenced on the east side February 13, 1886, with hand drills. Air drills took over June 18 after the arrival of compressor boilers, which was the first machinery to be used. Average daily progress with hand drills was 3.52 lineal feet; with air drills, 5.8 lineal feet. Hand drills started on the west end on April 1, 1886, and air drills, September 1, 1886.

Meanwhile, a campaign had arisen in Congress for forfeiture of "unearned" land grants. To ensure that the NP did not lose any of its federal grant, early in 1887 NP President Harris decided to lay a temporary switchback line, with track zigzagging over the summit. Train service could then get through to Tacoma a year before the tunnel was due to be finished. The last spike in the switchback was driven on June 1, 1887, and a test train proceeded from Yakima to Tacoma on June 6. This run was successful, and scheduled train service over Stampede Pass began July 3.

Meanwhile, tunnel digging progressed and, by May 1888, drillers from each side were about to meet. The Bennett brothers offered $1,000 to the first man through, plus a steak dinner and whiskey for the crew on his side. Each team selected a tough little powder monkey, and on May 3, when a draft was felt after a blast, these representatives from each side dove in the hole. After much pushing and struggling, the man from the west tunnel was shoved through, bruised and bleeding, but triumphant.

Mrs. Sidney Bennett, wife of the superintendent, had been demanding to be the first person to pass through the mountain, or at least to be the first woman to do so. She was on the scene and, after the tussle between the two powder monkeys ended, she crawled into the hole. A lady of ample proportions, she became stuck and, with considerable effort, was pulled back out. Imbued with the same determination as her husband and brother-in-law, she would not give up that easily. She shed some undergarments and sent for a bucket of lard to coat her shoulders and hips. On the second try, the men on the west side pulled her through. According to the legend, she then announced, "The drinks, gentlemen, are on my husband."

When the first train went through the tunnel on May 27, Nelson Bennett had beaten the deadline by a scant seven days. The tunnel he and his men completed was found to have a variance of just one inch in 9,844 feet. To celebrate the achievement, Bennett is reputed to have thrown a bash for his crews, providing 100 turkeys, 241 cases of oysters, and 5,000 cigars.

Left: Before double track was added in 1915, there had been four additional telegraph stations on the "Mountain" between the stations at Easton and Lester to handle the original single track operations. Between Martin and Easton was Upham, and between Stampede and Lester were Borup, Kennedy, and Weston. With single-track operation, dispatchers needed these telegraphers to deliver orders to trains, when necessary, to change meeting points. After 1915, double tracks providing a separate track for trains in each direction, these stations no longer were required and were closed. (Martin and Stampede, however, remained open because of the tunnel's single track and the staff system between them.) They were similar to Stampede and Martin when it came to the austere, isolated living conditions. The bachelor operators at Borup had a little fun posing for this 1910 photo illustrating their plight. Telegraphers were proud of their union, the Order of Railroad Telegraphers, as this Borup picture shows. Similar photos were taken at many different stations, with the telegraphers holding signs saying "100% O.R.T." or "Solid O.R.T."

Supposedly, men who had worked in the tunnel for three months or more received a pass to anywhere on the railroad, with a new suit for the journey thrown in.

Telegraph stations were established on each side of the tunnel—Martin on the east and Stampede on the west. When double track was installed in 1912–15 up to Martin and to New Stampede, it was the responsibility of the telegrapher to have the switches properly lined for the remaining single-track, 3.6-mile segment between the two tunnel stations. An additional duty included delivering rubber face masks with a wet sponge, one for each crew member passing through the tunnel, in a bag attached to a hoop. The operator also was required to keep these white rubber "respirators" clean by using an abrasive soap called Sapolio. An electrically connected safety system later was installed to control movement on the single track, in which the telegrapher at the station where a train was entering the tunnel removed a metal staff from a machine in his station, which could only be done while the operator at the opposite station pressed a release button. Once a staff was removed, the machine was inactivated. The train crew carried the staff through the tunnel and threw it off at the opposite end, where it was inserted in that station's machine, reactivating the system. This safety procedure ensured that two opposite moving trains would not meet head-on in the tunnel or single track. In 1957 this system was replaced by centralized traffic control signals operated from Easton and the stations at Martin and Stampede subsequently were closed.

I first worked at Martin on June 19, 1944, and Stampede, January 22, 1945. I filled relief vacancies at both stations for the next seven years and finally bid in third trick (midnight to 8:00 A.M.) at Stampede on October 1, 1949. With my wife Cereta and toddler son Jim, I lived there until moving to Auburn on April 15, 1950. It was a good way to gain financially. Northern Pacific provided housing, fuel, and utilities.

During our time at Stampede, Cereta also had some memorable experiences. Because she was a telegrapher, she occasionally was asked to work the midnight shift at Martin when the regular operator needed a day off. Number 2, the *North Coast Limited*, would slow down at Stampede so she could scramble aboard the engine and then it slowed down again at Martin so she could jump off. After finishing the shift at 8:00 A.M., she caught a ride back to Stampede with Track Supervisor Matt Fioretti on his speeder.

In later years I returned on outings with my Boy Scout troop to both Stampede and Martin. The following pages show some of my photos from various years on the "Mountain."

Northern Pacific living quarters at places like Stampede could be described as spartan at best. Second trick telegrapher Herbert "Denny" Denzene and his wife Triva wanted something better, so Denny bought and erected a nice, two-story prefabricated house. We found a good photo location near their house for our 1949 Christmas card. It featured our 19-month-old son, Jim, who is wearing his Howdy Doody earmuffs, Denny Denzene, and operator Tom Melvin's dog, Archie. Denny was an NP veteran with a seniority date of June 26, 1920, six years before I was born.

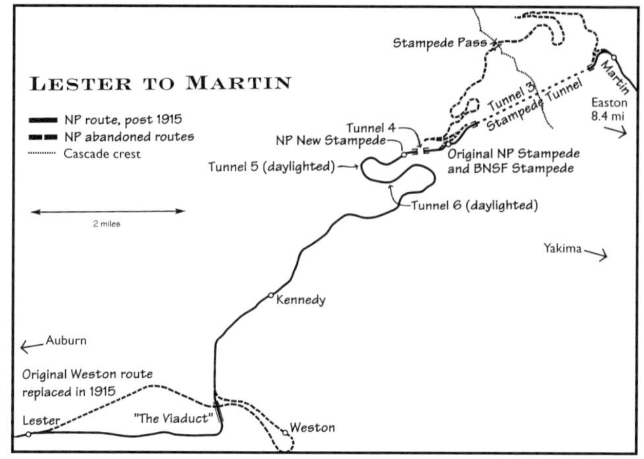

Map courtesy of CTC Board Railroads Illustrated

Northern Pacific fast freight Number 602 emerges from the east portal of Tunnel Number 4 at Stampede Pass in 1949. There are two tunnels in this 3.6-mile single-track segment between New Stampede and Martin. Located further east is Tunnel Number 3, the 9,844-feet-long Stampede tunnel whose east portal is at Martin. Tunnel Number 4 is 650 feet long, with its west portal at New Stampede Station. Old Stampede formerly stood in the mile of open space between the two tunnels. It was the location of the original station, school, and living quarters for the section crew, vent plant operators, and telegraphers except third trick, who lived in the back half of the New Stampede Station. New Stampede Station was established in 1914 at the end of the double track at the west portal of Tunnel 4.

Atop Tunnel 4 is a promontory with a stupendous view of the railroad where it passes through the Cascades summit. To the south is the Borup Loop, a two-mile-long horseshoe curve and almost a mile from one side to the other. From the upper side of the loop the track made another complete reversal of direction to come into New Stampede, then run through Tunnel 4 into Old Stampede. The whole show could be seen from this vantage point, my all-time favorite photo location.

I took my first photo from atop the promontory in June 1945 as day local passenger train Number 5 was about to enter Tunnel 4. The road locomotive is a class Q-6 Pacific type steam engine (4-6-2), which could pull five cars up the 2.2 percent mountain grade from Easton to Martin. On this day, Number 5 had six cars, one over the limit, and therefore had a new, four-unit class FT helper engine on the head end west to Lester. The snow shed in front of the tunnel entrance has water barrels on top for fire fighting. The vertical rails driven into the ground just to the left of the diesel are for snow slide protection in winter. Retired Roadmaster Bob Robey regards this as the most treacherous spot on the Mountain for slide trouble.

Number 5 has now left Tunnel 4 and is below the promontory at the east end of the two-mile long, S-shaped Borup Loop. The train is about to go under an old bridge on the Stampede to Lester forest service road. About the time of this photo (June 1945), this bridge was condemned and the road abandoned. Today the automobile road over Stampede Pass to Lester is located north of the railroad.

Number 5 is now on the south leg of the Borup Loop, directly across from my viewpoint. The consist includes a Railway Post Office car, baggage car, two coaches, café coach, and reserved seat coach. After leaving Lester, it will begin filling up with passengers going home to the Puget Sound area after a day of fishing on the Green River.

Same scene, 27 years later on August 8, 1972. Amtrak's Number 10, the *North Coast Hiawatha,* normally routed via Wenatchee, has been detoured through Stampede. There has been a dramatic growth in the forest plus the addition of a power line.

Left: Looking down on New Stampede Station in June 1945. Number 4, the eastbound *Alaskan,* is just about to go over the double track switch and enter Tunnel 4 on single track. It has double-header Class Q-6 engines, one of which is traveling east to bring back a troop train. Number 4 is on the eastward main track. The next track to the right is the westward main track, and adjacent to it is the westward siding. On the other side of the train is the eastward siding.

The engineer of the lead engine has his arm outstretched to pick up a hoop containing the staff and respirators. The station telegrapher, Cody Caldwell, has climbed up the little stairway to the "pulpit" to "hoop up." A little coal shed sits on this side of the station; most small stations on the Northern Pacific had coal-burning heating stoves. We would heave our garbage over the bank to the right of the train order signal, then watch bears rummaging for a treat.

Above: This view is from the engineer's cab of Train Number 4 as it approaches the tunnel. The telegrapher is standing on the "pulpit," ready to hoop up the staff for permission to go through the tunnel sections to Martin. The operator had used the staff to unlock the train order signal, which now indicates "proceed" for Number 4.

A blizzard paralyzed the Northwest on January 13, 1950. East-bound Number 602, which departed Lester with a four-unit FT road engine and four-unit FT helper cut back in the train, stalled in the snow just as it arrived at New Stampede. Another helper was sent up from Lester and succeeded in getting the train moving.

Train Number 603 glides through Old Stampede in January 1950. Deep snow made it difficult for me to find a place to stand with the camera. It reminds me of the prior December, when Engineer Ed Foisie asked me to cut a Christmas tree for him to pick up when he came through on Number 5. Because of seven-feet drifts, the best I could do was cut the top off a tree sticking up out of the snow. I was struggling through the snow with the tree just as the train arrived, and it took considerable effort to get it through the little, narrow diesel door. Good thing Ed was a fast runner, so he could make up for lost time.

This photo depicts the first of several Scout outings to Stampede Pass, on May 30, 1958. Assisted by Emery and Marian Coxen, I took nine members of Den 6, Tacoma Cub Scout Pack 118, on train Number 6 from East Auburn to Stampede. (The tenth member of the group was my son Tim, who was not yet old enough to be an official Cub Scout.) The time schedule was ideal with Number 6 arriving at 11:30 A.M., and departure on Number 5 at 4:00 P.M.

The boys have just detrained at Old Stampede and are being welcomed by the legendary Clementina Campanelli. She was the wife of "Boss" Sam, the section foreman, and was known for her culinary skills and strong spirit.

After disembarking, we hiked up to the Cascade crest to visit the U.S. Department of Commerce Weather Bureau station. From there, we continued a short distance to Lizard Lake for lunch. This is where Virgil Bogue's trail crew revolted, giving rise to the name Stampede Pass. The lake first was called Stampede Lake, then Monad Lake by Northern Pacific, and now is commonly known as Lizard Lake. The old, pre-tunnel switchback grade can be seen at top left.

The Scouts (*left to right*): Jim Fredrickson, Ted Johnson, Bobby Patten, Peter Pelligrene, Keith Wohlford, Ed Winskill, David Lewis, Tim Fredrickson, Brad Bryant, and John Mancini. Behind are Emery and Marian Coxen.

On January 31, 1959, I took Scout Executive Otto "Pat" Patten to Martin on Number 6 to inspect the Stampede area as a possible location for a permanent winter camp for Tacoma's Mount Rainier Council. Afterwards, we hiked on snowshoes over the Cascade crest to Stampede to catch Number 5 home. The temperature was 14° F, so we were thankful for a brief respite at the weather bureau buildings. The station stands on the dividing line between a moist Puget Sound climate and semi-desert central Washington. The building in the foreground served as living quarters, and instruments were located in the back building. In my days on the Mountain, the weather bureau staff hiked to or from Martin in the summer, or snowshoed in the winter, to make rail trips to civilization. No doubt snowmobiles are their primary mode of transportation nowadays.

Pat was enthusiastic about the potential for wilderness training here for Scouts. A tentative agreement was made between Northern Pacific and the Mount Rainier Council to lease land. Shortly afterwards, however, the whole deal fell through when it was announced that day trains 5 and 6 would be discontinued due to the loss of the mail contract *(see notice, right)*. With no means of transporting the Scouts, the dream died.

Loss of U.S. Mail forces NP to serve notice trains 5 & 6 will be discontinued

Northern Pacific operates daytime passenger Trains 5 and 6 between Seattle and Spokane primarily to accommodate travelers to and from intermediate stations, and to handle the mail.

Travel is comparatively light on these trains, but revenue from the mail has enabled us to hold losses on the operation to a minimum. We have been willing to absorb these losses in order to provide this service.

However, the Post Office Department has notified the Northern Pacific that under plans for postal service reorganization, railway post office service will be discontinued after March 31 on Northern Pacific Trains 5 and 6, on Trains 1 and 2 between Seattle and Spokane, and on highway post offices operated by the Northern Pacific Transport Company between Spokane and Lewiston, Idaho, and between Lewiston and Pasco, Washington.

This will result in a loss to Northern Pacific of more than $300,000 a year in mail revenue. Approximately $145,000 of that amount will be lost on Trains 5 and 6.

The sharp reduction in coach fares a few months ago has produced some increase in passenger business on these trains. However, resulting passenger revenue increases have been wholly insufficient and these operations have been conducted at a considerable loss. The mail revenue loss of $145,000 a year in addition to the existing deficit presents an intolerable situation.

Therefore, our only alternative is to notify the Washington Public Service Commission of our intention to discontinue Trains 5 and 6 between Seattle and Spokane on April 1, the date railroad post office service is to be discontinued on these trains.

We regret the necessity of taking this action, which will result in loss of jobs to railroad employes and loss of service to stations which only these trains serve. We will endeavor, where feasible, to adjust schedules of Trains 1 and 2 between Seattle and Spokane to serve as many of these stations as possible.

NORTHERN PACIFIC RAILWAY

"Drama Still Persists In Railroad Man's Life"

On December 2, 1967, I was riding in the cab of freight train Number 606 with engineer Ed Hurley and took this photo just before we entered two-mile-long Stampede Tunnel. The west portal view is not nearly as dramatic as the east portal at Martin, with its waterfall and steep cliff. The Puget Sound Power and Light substation at left supplied electricity for the ventilator fans housed atop the snowshed, out of sight in the photo.

An unusual event happened here on April 11, 1955, when I was working the midnight to 8:00 A.M. shift in Tacoma on the "Mountain" district. Herman Hunt was the police reporter for the Tacoma *News Tribune* and he had a small office in the County City building. Herman loved trains and would have preferred working for a railroad, but his father insisted that he do something better with his college education. For that reason, he ended up in journalism. Often, when something unusual happened on the NP, I would stop by Herman's office and fill him in. Sometimes this resulted in a *Tribune* story, as was the case on April 11. The headline and story follow:

DRAMA STILL PERSISTS IN RAILROAD MAN'S LIFE

The click and chatter of the telegraph key is gone—but there's still occasional melodrama in a railroad dispatcher's office. It happened in Tacoma again this Monday morning.

Most Tacoman's were still abed and the big office clock was leaning toward 5 a.m. while Chief Dispatcher Hal Bradbury and Trick Dispatcher Jim Fredrickson cast approving eyes over the night's train sheet. All seemed serene over the approximately 425 miles of the Northern Pacific's Tacoma division, from Portland, Yakima and Sumas.

The passenger trains were on time and freight trains making their "meets" without aggravation and nobody was getting "stabbed" unduly to wrinkle the brows of these watchful guardians who checked their movements.

The Portland passenger, 401, was scooting close to the Point Defiance tunnel and Second 679, a time freight was well ahead and into clear at Tacoma. No. 1, the westbound "Mainstreeter" was out of Ellensburg and right on the "advertised," under guidance of engineer Bob Still of Seattle in the big diesel cab and Conductor Burr Todd back in the coaches. A section of No. 602 time freight was nicely eastbound out of Auburn but the "meet" was not yet causing any problem.

Emergency Call Bobs Up

But suddenly a telephone jangled and Fredrickson heard the tense voice of an operator 77 miles away from snow-covered Stampede siding atop the Cascade Mountains. In terse sentences he told the story from his lonely station, banked on three sides with 74 inches of snow.

Two Seattle men, their small plane wrecked, he said, had scrambled several miles along the snowy wastes, braving cougars and bears despite the fact that both were slightly injured and going had been slow. The tiny yellow light glowing from the lonely station at the west end of the Stampede tunnel, had been their salvation.

Fredrickson turned to Chief Bradbury and explained. No local train would pass Stampede for hours and the lordly No. 1 usually coasted down the mountainside with scarcely a hooted diesel toot for the lonely depot.

Fast Train to Rescue

Bradbury went into immediate action, preparing an order immediately dispatched to the plushy limited at Martin, on the east end of the two-mile tunnel. It commanded Engineer Still and Conductor Todd to halt their fast train and to pick up the injured men and take them to Seattle.

That's the way it happened.

The Tacomans didn't know the names of the Seattle men or the story of their mishap. They only know they—and the Stampede operator—did what was required. It was just part of the job, they said.

All I had told Herman was that the plane had crashed and we had stopped Number 1 to pick up the two grounded men. He had reconstructed all of the rest of the story from his personal knowledge of the division. The one part not quite right regarded where the two men were picked up. They had made their way down to the west portal of Stampede Tunnel and entered the ventilator plant, which at that time was operated by remote control from New Stampede Station. They had a little trouble figuring out how to work the block phone between the vent plant and the station, but finally discovered the little push button needed to activate it. They contacted the telegrapher who in turn informed me of the situation.

The *Seattle Times* also ran a front page story with red headlines—"Two Men Crash-Land Plane In Cascades, Hike 5 Hours to Safety" and gave the names of the fliers: Allen Dickerson and Roy Prater of Seattle.

Right: The message to train Number 1, written on a "pad of clip" in my handwriting:

Q 11th No 1 RT
Stop at Vent Plant at Stampede & load psgrs who were injured in airplane crash. These psgrs will be at top of stairway ~~landing~~ which is next to vent plant inside of the snow shed and it will be probably be necessary for you to help them down this stairway. Section 4 man at SI should be on hand to show you where to spot coach.

Q = Tacoma
RT = Martin
SI = Stampede

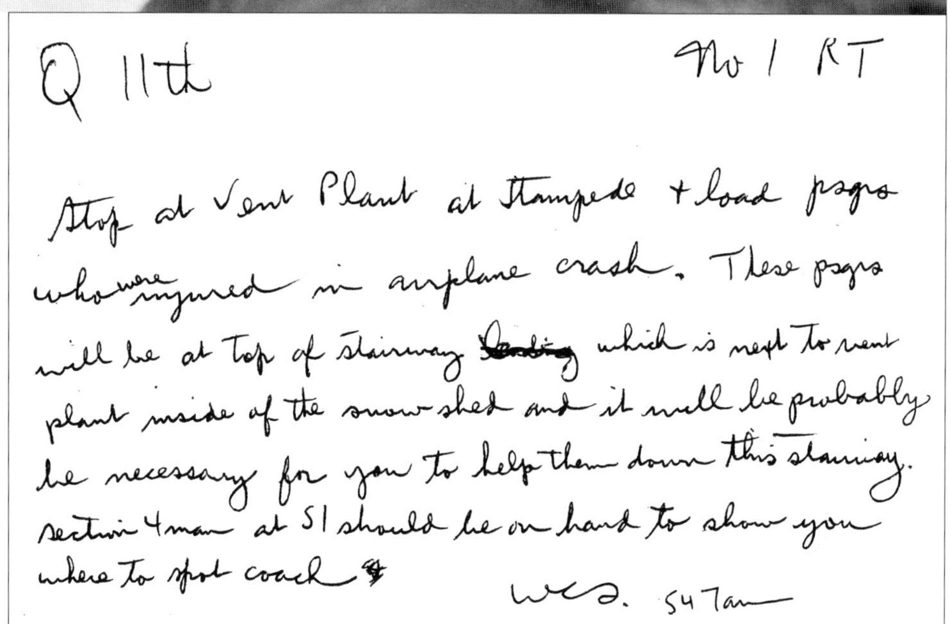
Q 11th No 1 RT

Stop at Vent Plant at Stampede + load psgrs who were injured in airplane crash. These psgrs will be at top of stairway ~~landing~~ which is next to vent plant inside of the snow shed and it will be probably be necessary for you to help them down this stairway. section 4 man at SI should be on hand to show you where to spot coach

WCS. 547am

A summertime view of Martin showing where the track enters the snowshed, which curves to the tunnel at the right of the waterfall. When tunnel digging commenced in 1886, the Mosquito Creek waterfall was diverted to the left to make way for the excavation.

The buildings at left included the third trick operator's quarters (box car), a duplex for second and first trick operators, a house belonging to section man Amobilio Innocenti, and, finally, the depot.

At right is a footbridge crossing the gulch to the old switchback grade that could be used by automobiles until snow fell. One night, while driving to work before midnight, I stuck my 1933 Studebaker Rockne in a ditch. I hiked the last mile into Martin with no flashlight, anxiously wondering how many bears might be lurking in the bushes. A tunnel spur leads off the westward siding on the far right, with a company service boxcar standing at the far end.

A westbound freight pulled by Class Z-3 engine 4015, a 2-8-8-2 compound Mallet, waits near Martin Station in 1944 for its turn to enter the Stampede Tunnel. Days are numbered for this poor old "Sow" and its sisters, who had labored valiantly for so many years lugging trains over Stampede Pass. The first diesel-electric locomotive had just come to the Tacoma Division in April 1944.

The 4015 was built in 1914, and scrapped at the South Tacoma shops, September 19, 1945. Behind 4015 sits a Northern Pacific cattle car and a Milwaukee Road ice bunk refrigerator car—both types, too, became victims of "progress."

On this Boy Scout outing in January 1960, I wanted to get one last photo of Martin Station before it was torn down. I crossed Mosquito Creek gulch to the old switchback grade where I had this nice, open view. Memories abound for me at this special place.

Rail Folks

Edna St. Vincent Millay once wrote:

> My heart is warm with the friends I'll make
> And the friends I'll not be knowing,
> But there isn't a train I would not take,
> No matter where it's going.

So many people love trains. Rail fans abound worldwide as evidenced by the Northern Pacific Railway Historical Association, which has members in Australia, England, Germany, and Africa, as well as the United States. Their interests in railroading vary widely. Some like trains in general; others, locomotives; while rolling stock and structures, especially stations, are the focus of numerous people. However, I don't know of many who are fans of those who make the whole show go—the railroad worker. I can say that I have enjoyed everything about being a railroader, particularly the people I have worked with and known.

"Rails" have a language of their own. Almost every railroad occupation has its peculiar nickname, and often more than one. Here are some of the in-house names for railway people:

Brakeman—shack, stinger (a student is a scissor bill)
Car repairman—car knocker, car toad
Clerk in freight yard—mud hop
Clerk in office—pencil pusher
Company doctor—croaker
Conductor—brains, captain, conducer
Dispatcher—delayer, detainer
Employee riding on pass—deadhead
Engineer—hoghead, hogger, eagle eye, throttle artist (also ballast scorcher, if runs fast)
Fireman—ashcat, bakehead, tallowpot, coal heaver, fire boy
Hobo—bindle stiff, box car tourist
Official—brass hat (plural: the brass)
Railroader with many years of service—old head
Restaurant waitress—beanery queen
Special agent (police)—cinder dick, flatfoot, gumshoe, yard bull
Superintendent—old man
Switchman—snake
Telegrapher—brasspounder, lightning slinger
Yardmaster—ringmaster

Railroaders who drifted from one road to another were called "boomers," whereas those who stayed put for their careers were regarded as "home guard." The lingo relating to firemen has faded away with the coming of diesels and no doubt other colorful names will be the victims of modern technology as well. I have mentioned only the names related to people. Almost everything else on the railroad has a slang term, too.

I should have taken many more photos of "rails" on the job, but fortunately I have enough to rekindle many fond mermories.

The 2.2 percent mountain grade climb over Stampede Pass extends 10 miles from Lester to Stampede going east, and 8.4 miles from Easton to Martin when proceeding west. Before diesel power took over, most passenger trains required one or two helper steam engines, and full tonnage freight trains always needed two helper engines to surmount this obstacle. This required a substantial work force to be assigned at both Lester and Easton. Each helper steam engine required an engineer and fireman, and every train with helpers had a conductor-pilot to shepherd them. There were roundhouses at both stations, with foremen and a staff of machinists, as well as laborers to shovel coal cinders. Each station also had a coal dock and a water tank to be maintained. Diesel locomotives drastically reduced the need for helper engines, which finally were eliminated altogether. This in turn shut down the roundhouses. The stations at Lester, Stampede, Martin, and Easton have long been abandoned; all that remains is a track maintenance section crew at Easton.

This photo, taken at Easton in June 1945, is representative of the great people it took to move trains over the Mountain. *From left to right:*

Engineer **Herbert "Pop" Saunders** was born in Purpon-wils, England, but spent most of his life in far away Lester, Washington, as helper engineer for the Northern Pacific. He acquired the most magnificent house in Lester, a mansion built by lumber baron E.G. Morgan. "Pop" raised dairy cows and had a milk business as a sideline, and the Morgan logging operation was his biggest customer. The Morgan mansion became his in a settlement for unpaid milk bills— the result of mill fires and other financial problems.

Velta Mae Sparkman was raised in Oklahoma, but her family moved to Washtucna to work on a wheat farm. After graduating from high school, "Sparky" intended to enter business school in Spokane. While rooming at the YWCA, someone told her there was a telegraph school right around the corner, much closer than the business school. That sounded good to her, so she enrolled. After graduating, she was sent to Northern Pacific's Tacoma Division where she worked as a telegrapher at various stations, including Easton. It was there that she met Warren Graybeal, a roundhouse machinist who had grown up in Easton, where his family operated a grocery store and service station. They were married and then moved to Oklahoma to be near her family.

Dutch Manicke was a native of Lester, where his father was a fire cleaner in the roundhouse. After high school, he began a lifelong career with the Northern Pacific as a locomotive fireman and then engineer. His brother Tony, who worked in the Stampede vent plant when I worked at Stampede, reported that the crews "thought the world" of Dutch.

Trainmen and enginemen had the "glamour jobs" on the railroad, but they could not have moved their trains without the collaborative efforts of many people— telegraphers, yardmasters, clerks, and other "non-operating" employees. This photo represents some of these folks, taken at the Auburn yard office in 1944. On the left is Yardmaster **Ray Bolton,** in charge of all of the switching in this vast classification yard, where inbound trains were taken apart and outbound trains made up. **Hazel Boyce** is the inbound clerk, processing the consists of trains coming into the yard. She received this information by both telegraph and telephone from the yards where the trains originated.

Yardmasters were notorious for their colorful vocabulary; Ray was a master.

Hazel, a native of Vermont, never lost her New England accent. When a freight train arrived at Auburn, yard clerks tacked small cards on the sides of the cars to indicate their ultimate destination in Seattle, Tacoma, or branch line stations. These cards were prepared in advance from the train consists, and Hazel dictated the information to whomever was available to write it down. When it was time to fill out the cards, she shouted in her distinctive Northeastern accent, "Cawd writahs!" and all who were not otherwise occupied would assemble. It was not one of my duties as a telegraph operator to write cards, but if free, I joined the group anyhow, because it was fun!

World War II brought in an influx of young people to the railroad. I was 16 years old when I went to work as a call boy at Tacoma Union Station for the Northern Pacific, and the four young ladies in the photo were in the same age bracket. *Left to right:* **Bev Skaugsett, Bev Davis, Elaine Rogers,** and **Bev Roller.**

Bev Davis led the parade, going to work at the Union Station restaurant in June 1942, at age 16. Originally, when the station was opened in 1911, there had been a large dining room, but during the Depression this space was taken over by the Division Superintendent's staff. A lunch counter was installed just off the concourse, with a few tables at the far end. This was managed by NP's dining car department. Manager Jenny Morgan was allowed to hire Bev Davis, and told that if the girl was successful, more persons of her age could be employed. She worked as a waitress and cashier, and did Jenny's accounting and typing. As Bev passed the test, two more of her Lincoln High School friends, Bev Skaugsett and Elaine Rogers, also were hired to work at the restaurant. Eventually, all three of them went downstairs to the dispatcher's office to fill some clerical positions. Elaine became a crew caller and the two Bevs ended up on the night shift. As night clerk, Bev Davis worked the awful hours of 2:00 A.M. to 10 A.M. and was responsible for the "morning report"—a long, detailed account for the division officials that showed the performance of most of the previous day's trains and included the delays. The report was compiled from the six dispatchers' train sheets, on which they kept their records of train movements. The night clerk also received a copy of delay reports made by the dispatchers for each scheduled train, in order to transmit them to headquarters in St. Paul, Minnesota.

Bev Skaugsett worked a second night clerk job, involving the complex passenger operations brought about by the movements of large numbers of World War II troop trains.

Bev Roller, from my own Stadium High School, entered railroad service as the result of a tip from a family friend, who worked at Union Station. She was assigned to the third trick caller position.

Thus, there were three Bevs on the same shift in the dispatcher's office. Understandably, when Night Chief Dispatcher R.B. Lewis called out, "Bev," confusion resulted—until he hit upon his "three vitamin" solution: the three young women became "B-1," "B-2," and "B-3"!

When my family and I moved out of Stampede in April 1950, a boxcar was provided for our household goods on the Cle Elum to Auburn local freight. The train stopped with this boxcar, opposite to the New Stampede Station where we lived, and the crew loaded our furniture and other belongings. Then they posed in the snow for a group photo. *Left to right:* Engineer **Art Westborg;** Fireman **Ernie Olin;** Brakemen **John Duncan, Charlie Larson, Bobbie Bartro;** and Conductor **Oscar Duncan.** For me, working for the Northern Pacific felt like being part of a big, happy family.

About a year after the Burlington Northern merger, BN embarked on a program to send train dispatchers out on the road for a close-up look at the territory they were controlling. Previously, dispatchers wanting to "learn the road" had to do so on their own time, without pay, and would hitch a ride in a locomotive in their district. Now, a trainmaster was assigned to take groups of dispatchers out in a "hi-rail" automobile, so called because it was equipped to travel on either highways or rails. On April 4, 1971, five of us started out at King Street Station in Seattle with Trainmaster Jerry Bergman in a BN Checker sedan to see part of the north end branches. At Woodinville, we stopped in a good spot for a group photo.

Left to right:

Tom Moore had a high school friend tell him that he had overheard an NP agent in a restaurant say he was short of help at the freight house. Tom immediately applied and went to work as a "mud hop" in the freight yard. He didn't care much for that line of work and signed up for the NP telegraph school in Jamestown, North Dakota. After graduating in 1944, he started as a telegrapher "bucking the extra list" and worked many stations over the Tacoma Division. He was at Auburn Depot in 1960. Being a very talented telegrapher, he was promoted to train dispatcher.

Jerry Bergman graduated with me from Tacoma's Stadium High School in 1945. (While there, we formed a railroad club.) Jerry had about as colorful a career as anyone could have. He started at NP as a roundhouse laborer in Tacoma in 1943, then hostler helper, and next yard clerk. From 1945 to 1948, he served his country in the United States Navy before coming back to the railroad. Just as he returned, he filled a vacancy as a stenographer to Division Superintendent Thomas J. Kane. From there he went to Missoula, Montana, as a track apprentice, followed by appointment as assistant roadmaster at Livingston. After that, he was named assistant trainmaster at Spokane. Then came trainmaster assignments at Duluth, Minnesota; Jamestown, North Dakota; and Centralia, Washington. From 1965 to 1966, Jerry worked in Seattle as assistant to the general manager of lines west of Livingston. Then he served as trainmaster at Auburn until 1973, when he was appointed assistant division superintendent in Spokane. In 1978 he was sent to Denver to be terminal superintendent, followed by promotion to division superintendent in Lincoln, Nebraska. He eventually returned to Seattle as general superintendent of transportation, and ended his successful railroad career as division superintendent in Springfield, Missouri. He retired in 1982.

Paul Thompson might have been considered a "boomer" in the old days. He was from Ohio and had worked for a number of Midwest railroads before migrating west to the NP, first as telegrapher and then dispatcher in Tacoma.

"Long John" Haakonson graduated from Anacortes High School in 1955 and shortly thereafter noticed ads in the paper for the Spokane Telegraph School. He decided to give telegraphy a try, since he had found trains fascinating. (He had made trips to the Seattle Roundhouse with future Northern Pacific Historical Association president Gary Tarbox to photograph steam engines.) When completing telegraphy school in April 1956, "Long John" already had been notified of a need for operators in Tacoma. He served as one of the last operators at 15th Street Tower in Tacoma before it was replaced by an electronic control system. Showing an immediate aptitude for railroading, in a little over a year he was promoted to train dispatcher in Tacoma. "Long John" spent 1960 and 1961 in the Army, where he served as a radio-teletype operator. In 1973 he left the railroad and went to work for Georgia Pacific in Bellingham, near his old home.

Don Shane was a jack of all trades, and master of most of them. After discharge from the Navy in 1946, he tried working as an automobile mechanic, but didn't care much for that line of work, and consequently responded to an ad for the Spokane Telegraph School. He enrolled under the GI Bill, and after graduating was hired by NP Chief Dispatcher Austin Ackley as a Tacoma Division telegrapher. After working at a number of stations, he decided to respond to an offer from the Navy for former sailors to come back in at their old rate (he had been an Aviation Radioman Third Class). After resigning from the Northern Pacific, however, he got cold feet about reentering the Navy, backed out before raising his right hand, and went to Spokane where he hired on with the Great Northern as a pipefitter at the Hillyard shops. Next Don transferred to become a brakeman, but found he didn't care much for the irregular hours. He quit and attended a watchmaking school in Los Angeles. After completion of this training he found work repairing watches in Bremerton, but that profession, too, was not to his liking. Don returned to the NP in Tacoma, and once again Mr. Ackley hired him as a telegrapher and later promoted him to dispatcher. Don and I worked many a third trick together in the dispatcher's office in Union Station.

244
Punch somebody in Miami.
General Telephone
WASHINGTON
OTK 266

This photo, taken at the Central Building in Seattle in May 1981, shows Burlington Northern Regional Material Manager **Wilhelm Schlieper** and his secretary, **June Peterson.** Bill was one of the most fascinating people I ever met on the railroad. He had been a U-boat sailor in the German Navy during World War II and commented on how lucky he was to be alive. Only about ten percent survived. His submarine was bombed when coming into Wilhelmshaven, and half the crew perished. He was in the lucky half that made it to shore. After the war, he immigrated to the United States and went to live with an aunt in Brainerd, Minnesota, who found a job for him at the Northern Pacific's large repair shops. He went to work in the material department, and rose through the ranks until he was assistant manager at Brainerd. From there, he went to Laurel, Montana, to serve as material manager, before being promoted to head the material department for the Seattle-Portland Region for Burlington Northern in Seattle. I was working in the Central Building in the Transportation Department and we became good friends, partly because my son Tim was a nuclear submarine officer in the United States Navy. Once, when Tim was in Seattle, the three of us went to lunch. Afterwards Bill commented that he had felt just a little uncomfortable sitting at the same table with an officer, for in the German Navy no such fraternizing ever would have occurred between officers and enlisted men. He was an absolutely delightful person, and it is very sad that he fell victim to cancer about six months before he was due to retire.

June Peterson has been a friend of mine since coming to work for the Northern Pacific in 1963 as a stenographer in the Tacoma dispatcher's office. She then went to the South Tacoma shops as stenographer to the chief clerk, and then to the material department. After the merger, she went to Seattle as secretary to the material manager—first Dick Liljenberg and then Wilhelm Schlieper. June also became president of our Northern Pacific Veterans Club.

Over the years I have been the photographer at many happy occasions, when my friends and fellow workers have retired. The usual pattern began with a coffee and cake hour at Union Station in Tacoma, followed by a formal retirement dinner at a restaurant. On July 31, 1978, we gathered in the superintendent's office to honor Jimmie Wyse, an immensely popular person who was held in high regard by all who knew and worked with him. Being around Jimmie made everyone smile, as the photo shows.

Front row left to right: **Clayton McLean, Tom Moore, Jimmie Wyse**
Back row: Chief Dispatcher **Chuck Stillman, John Ackley, Duke Tone, Frank Ryan, Ken Iverson, Dave Steinhoff,** and **Jim Fredrickson**. (Someone held my camera and clicked the shutter for this picture.)

Jimmie's father, L.C. Wyse, went to work for the NP as a telegrapher in 1910, and Jimmie spent his younger years in the living quarters at the Adna Station on the South Bend Branch. Jimmie's date as a telegrapher was 1937.

A Tribute to Fellow Railroad Photographers

Left to right: **Albert Farrow, Jim Fredrickson,** and **Warren McGee** at Ellensburg in 1990 to photograph steam engine SP&S 700, which was built to Northern Pacific class A-3 plans. The late Walt Grande, noted SP&S historian, took the picture.

From 1940 onward, I eagerly awaited each month for the latest issue of the two prominent publications devoted to trains and rail fans, *Railroad Magazine* and *Trains,* always hoping to find photos of the Northern Pacific. When they appeared, the credit line most likely would read "photo by Ronald Nixon," "...Warren McGee," or "...Albert Farrow." Ronald was a train dispatcher in Missoula, Warren a conductor in Livingston, and Albert a locomotive engineer in Auburn. Not only were they masters of their profession, they also possessed a remarkable talent for photographing trains, locomotives, and everything else related to railroading. Shortly after starting my railroad career, as a call boy in Tacoma in 1943, I made a pilgrimage to Montana to search out Nixon and McGee—with fifty percent success. Nixon made me feel most welcome in Missoula, while McGee was far away in the Pacific on Guadalcanal. I was forced to wait a couple years before McGee could indoctrinate me in the wonders of Livingston, his heaven on earth. Shortly after my first session as a telegrapher at Auburn Yard, I was able to meet Albert Farrow, who was on one of the trains going though the yard.

It not only was a pleasure being able to meet these famous photographers, but we instantly commenced enduring friendships. Ronald Nixon and Albert Farrow are no longer with us, but I remain in close touch with Warren McGee and we continue to chase trains together. Just can't break the habit.

Index